ARCHITECTURE OF TODAY

E. Saarinen: General Motors Technical Centre, near Detroit

USA

UDO KULTERMANN

ARCHITECTURE OF TODAY

A SURVEY OF NEW BUILDING THROUGHOUT THE WORLD

UNIVERSE BOOKS NEW YORK

Translated by E.H.W. Priefert

© 1959 by Verlag Ernst Wasmuth, Tübingen.
Library of Congress Catalog Card Number: 59–7234.
Printed in Germany.

CONTENTS

FOREWORD

An architectural work of art can only be understood and interpreted "in the round". Illustrations give merely shadowy indications of its reality, which is impossible to experience either from photographs or even from theoretical study.

The photographs selected for this book cannot therefore present the individual buildings adequately; also, plans and detail drawings which would have explained the structures themselves better than photographs have been purposely omitted. The chief aim has been to show the continuity and the convincing quality of the international architecture of the present and to view these as part of a living tradition. The pictures were chosen to exhibit the essential tendencies of modern architecture, rather than to give a comprehensive survey. Thus some buildings considered milestones in the process of development, are sometimes shown in two illustrations, whereas some other masterpieces of modern architecture are only mentioned in the text. This is not meant as an evaluation. The attempt has merely been made to render visible in each separate chapter the general tendencies of development from the disciplined structural frame to the new freedom of dynamic spatial conceptions. Furthermore one of the most important aims was to show the leading position of contemporary architecture among the arts.

I should like here sincerely to thank all those architects and photographers, the cultural attachés of the various embassies and the publishers who have so generously supported my endeavors. My special thanks are due to Herr Günther Wasmuth for his understanding furtherance of my work.

U. K.

FUNDAMENTAL PRINCIPLES

The architecture of the past hundred years can be considered as a completed phase in a stylistic historical development. Since about 1950 there have been added new technical and artistic architectural forms indicating a new approach to design. They form part of the historical continuity which links them with the achievements of former centuries. They are the result, as it were, of an integration of organic and crystalline form elements, which combine in a spatial effect of a new order. The tasks imposed on the architect by the community have altered with the political and social changes. Technical discoveries and industrial advances have created fundamentally new conditions. The main criteria of architecture, however, have remained the same throughout all the phases of historic development, namely the realizations of creative imagination from space and volume, light and shadow, rhythmic tension and balance.

Up to the end of the 18th century wood and stone were the decisive building materials. The works of the graphic arts, murals, frescoes, plaster work and sculpture were inseparable components of the architectural organism. The main task of architecture was to manifest the cultural aspirations of a small class of people. Churches and monasteries, great country houses, the seats of the aristocracy, had been style-setters for all types of buildings since the middle ages. Individual houses of ordinary citizens and the whole townscape were for centuries subordinated to these representational buildings. The beginning and standard of all was man with his increasing understanding of life and the world. The architectural vocabulary (column, pilaster and gable) corresponded to the proportions of the human body.

The development of more recent architecture shows a decisive change. Through the French Revolution the privileges of a small ruling class had been in principle eliminated and each individual endowed with equal rights. The social levelling is reflected even in architecture since that time. The work of the architect is no longer subservient to the power of the ruling classes, but rather the needs of the general public. This social change as well as transition to an economic structure serving the indeterminate market and the concentration of population in large towns originated new types of architectural tasks, giving rise to typical forms: the museum for the public; the railway station for the speedier movement of the masses; the department store which offers a wide choice to the industrial worker; the exhibition building for the international exchange of industrial and cultural products; the factory as the place of work of a proletariat pressing for emancipation; the apartment houses and the housing development for all classes of society; hospitals; schools; buildings for sport and community centers for social and cultural use by the general public; and lastly town planning as the co-ordination of all creative and social activities and aspirations in one comprehensive order for the community.

In studying the emergence of these new building problems, a tendency towards a widening of the scope for art in the approach to basic design is evident. At the same time the striving for representation in increasing measure is replaced by a functional design catering for the basic requirements of the highest possible number of people. Only by acknowledging existing necessities could these architectural tasks be acknowledged and considered afresh. Before 1800 there were neither schools, hospitals, nor dwellings which were designed in principle with a view to their appropriate function, but they were buildings of uniform character which happened to be used as an educational establishment, infirmary or dwelling-house.

Naturally decisive changes also resulted from the discovery of new materials. The use of iron in the structure of a building, at first in a hidden position, and later on quite freely exposed, offered possibilities of construction which opened up new fields of exploration in the realm of design. It was not a mere coincidence that the first steps on this road were made by bridge designers, technical experts and structural engineers, who were able to experiment without any historical bias. Without representational or artistic preconceptions tasks were mastered which came into being through the altered conditions of the times, such as bridges, storehouses and harbor installations. In these cases no other solution was sought for, than the one resulting from the greatest economy of materials and finance. From there the development continued in various streams towards a stylistic language which at first made the new materials and more recently the structure itself the aesthetic principle, ornamental elaborations being completely discarded.

Side by side with the widening of the artistic possibilities, and supported by the specific properties of the new materials, was the endeavor to simplify the elements and to limit the number of different materials to the minimum.

A new unifying principle had to be found as the scope of architectural tasks widened. This was afforded in ideal measure by the new building materials. The steel frame permitted the elimination of load bearing walls and the wall of glass resulted in the curtain wall construction.

Standardization and rhythmic repetition of proportions took the place of individual and organic diversity. Simple massing and emphasis of the structure became artistic factors. The shell construction already tested during the 19th century and the latest experiments with space frames no longer differentiate between support and load, roof and wall, framework and ornament. Rather are they complex creations in which each part has a function intimately connected with the whole. The modern shell constructions and suspended parabolic roofs can be compared with the canopy room of the Byzantine churches. The decisive architectural principle in both cases is determined by a system of roof construction and load bearing stanchions. The wall is no longer an integral part of the total form; its function of dividing rooms has been eliminated. Other significant factors in matters of style, such as non-static composition, pre-eminence of plain surfaces in a building, and dimensions extended apparently into infinity can be added to this comparison. Our age has given a legitimate architectural expression to its inherent driving forces, the demand for order, fascination, social harmony and structural audacity.

In other realms of artistic creation similar fundamental transformations can be observed. In the graphic arts there has taken place since the 19th century a complete change which is likewise determined by new media subject to laws of their own and by new pictorial tasks.

In the works of Paul Cézanne this attitude can be compared already in a classical form with the achievements of the past. In it the transformation of realistic picture has been achieved which both acknowledges universal values and expresses each aspect of visible actuality through the power of the artist's imagination. Cubism and neo-plasticism, suprematism and the "absolute" painting of Kandinsky continue to extend the theme while re-orientating the pictorial media. In recent years a reaction against this attitude has come about. The new painting of dynamic forces, the dynamizing and revaluation of color as a means of expression and of magic spatial value, call the conventional kinds of painting into question. Labels like tachism, "un art autre", brutalism and abstract expressionism try to describe this phenomenon. Pollock, Dubuffet, Wols and Mathieu are the exponents of this movement, the aims of which are comparable with the architectural works of Lafaille, Nowicki, Saarinen and Candela. It is the fascination of the dynamic approach that they have in common.

In the sculptural realm also the main task of the artist since Brancusi, Gonzalez and Calder is no longer the strictly individualistic work but the universal one, that is, the artist is in his fundamental forms of expression only the medium for a message which is far beyond his own horizon of perception. The majority of sculptors who dominate the present situation are creating forms and abstractions of enhanced power of expression in the sense of a massing of solids or space transcending mysticism. The pictorial work radiates a message which goes beyond the purely personal and is reduced to geometric or elemental figures. An integration of sculpture with the social structure cannot be envisaged either by the creation of symbolic monuments or by its relation to architecture and town planning.

Even from literature and music, the two most personal sectors of the arts, man as a perspective individual is being eliminated. The three-dimensional interpretation of psychological sensations, and their integration in a composition that is a law to itself, place these creations among those which express universality. In literature the most decisive works are those of Kafka, Joyce and Pound, on whose foundation lately the French dramatists Beckett, Adamov and Ionesco and the German lyricists Heissenbüttel and Gomringer have been continuing. The magic attraction of the world of the theatre has been given a new evaluation by the drama. In lyrical works the language is not only the medium for voicing personal or subconscious urges, but constitutes the substance with which to build a magic reality independent of man.

Music has been released in part from the human interpreter's rôle of intermediary, and one experiments with pure tones and new rhythms, building on the life-work of Arnold Schönberg and Anton von Webern in electronic music and musique concrête, and on Edgar Varese and the dadaist composers. There are also dynamic elements dormant in the compositions by Nono, Stockhausen and Boulez, which expand contemporary music to celestial dimensions. Sounds moving through space with predetermined direction result in modifications of the musical note, a thing which has only become possible in this highly technical present age. "Contemporary music moves between the accidental and the directional as the extremes", as Herbert Eimert has said.

There are no breaks in living development. They are only aids for the orderly mind of the historian. The perpetual lament about the crisis and the transitional character of an age is only derived from inaptitude to discern historical flux. Every current age can and must be directly experienced in its artistic manifestations too. The plea that only past epochs can be assessed correctly, whereas contemporary works of art are exempted from an evaluation, merely shows the lack of ability to see the specifically artistic element, even of the past. After all, any historical consideration can only start from the present age and from its newly created assessments of value and interpretation.

When one considers the avenues of development of contemporary architecture leading from the present scene, the products of the 19th century are given a new evaluation. The brilliant imaginations of Ledoux and Schinkel; the works of engineering by Telford, Paxton, Labrouste, Contamin and Eiffel; the arts and crafts movement starting with Ruskin and Morris; the educational influence of Semper and Viollet-le-Duc; the buildings of the British architects Mackintosh, Macmurdo and Voysey; and the buildings of McKim, Mead and White, Sullivan, Le Baron Jenney, Burnham and Root, Holabird and Roche and Frank Lloyd Wright are milestones in the creative development of modern architecture. A large number of the buildings of these engineers and architects can already be described as modern. Around 1900 the ideas latent in the 19th century mature and develop in many countries independently of each other. Holland dissociated itself from the traditional architecture and with Berlage and the succeeding group of Oud, Rietveld, van Tijen, Maaskant, Duiker and Dudok, blossoms out with its architecture which closely reflects social reality. Austria made important strides towards a new order of architectural means of expression with Wagner, Loos and Hoffmann. Belgium laid the foundations of a dynamic trend in architecture with the "Jugendstil"

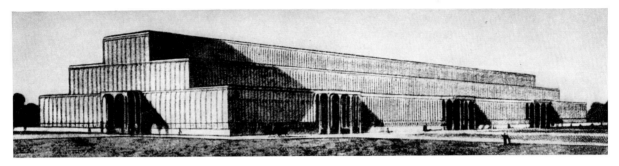

J. Paxton: Design for the Crystal Palace, London

J. Paxton: Crystal Palace, London, 1851 Exhibition

Luis Sullivan: Department Store, Chicago

J. M. Olbrich: "Hochzeits-Turm", Darmstadt

A. Gaudi: "Casa Milá", Barcelona

H. Gumard: Underground Station, Paris

V. Horta: "Maison du Peuple", Brussels

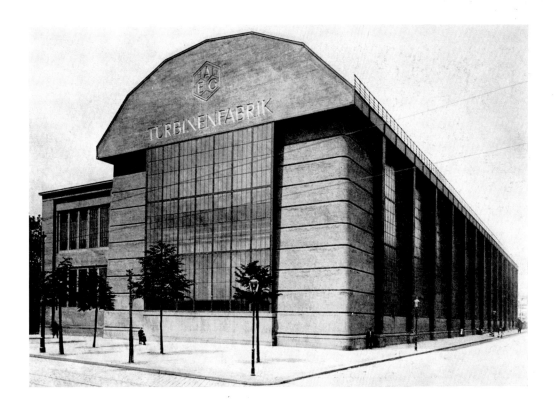

Peter Behrens: Turbine Hall
of the AEG, Berlin

Walter Gropius: Machine Hall, "Werkbund" Exhibition, Cologne, 1914

Walter Gropius: The "Bauhaus" at Dessau, near Leipzig

S. Leonidoff: Design for the Lenin Institute, Moscow

through Horta, Hankar and van de Velde. In Spain Gaudi created visionary forms, using new effects of texture and materials which anticipated expressionist architecture.

The movement in Germany, which started relatively late, resulted in starting the "Werkbund" and with it the systematic fight for the synthesis of technical and artistic results. This movement was begun by Messel, Tessenow, Behrens, Poelzig and Berg. The latent tendencies of the new movement were brought out into full daylight in the works of Gropius, Bruno and Max Taut, Mies van der Rohe, Mendelsohn, Scharoun and Häring, and especially in the work of the Bauhaus. France followed through Le Corbusier to new architectural trends in conjunction with the brilliant early achievement of Perret and Garnier. These side by side with the Bauhaus became the second great force in the pursuits of the new movement.

The twenties of this century were decisive in the unfolding of the architectural achievements in the countries mentioned above and for laying the foundations of a new methodical approach to architectural design. In addition these years saw the opening up of new countries which since that time have had an influence on international development: thus, for instance, Scandinavia through the works of Aalto, Asplund, Markelius and Jacobsen; Italy through Terragni, Gardella, Trucco and Nervi; Brazil through Warchavchik and Costa; Japan through Ymada, Yoshida, Mayekawa and Sakakura. Great Britain after a considerable interval rejoined the international development through the works of Lubetkin, Skinner, E. Maxwell Fry, Yorke, Rosenberg and Mardall. In Switzerland, a number of younger architects liberated themselves from the prevailing "Heimat" architecture. Furthermore the Eastern European countries aroused the interest of the world public. The brilliant designs of the Russian architects Leonidoff and Vesnin sought to exploit the specific structures of glass and steel and are fascinating through their audacious and completely novel dynamic effects. Czechoslovakia and Yugoslavia took up the ideas of the avant-garde and modified them according to their social needs.

The twenties saw the world-wide spread of those ideas, which in Great Britain, France, Germany and the United States had been under discussion for decades. It is no accident that by 1930 in many countries quite independently the name "international architecture" had been suggested for the entire movement which, though modified according to topographical conditions, had spread all over the world. From the nineteen-thirties until the end of World War II, this development was interrupted in a number of countries. In fact only North and South America, Sweden and Switzerland during that time achieved an organic progression.

After 1945 the U.S.A., which had attracted important personalities of the avant-garde during the struggles for power and the political differences in Europe, became of central importance for architecture. There the educational activity of the great pioneers, who came not only from Europe, but also from other continents, showed striking results.

In Europe the balance of power has shifted slightly. France and Germany, who suffered from the results of the war and from missed opportunities in town planning are still the receivers rather than the givers of style. Finland, the Scandinavian countries and Northern Italy are now countries with a promising development. In comparison, Holland, Belgium and Great Britain have gone backwards. In Poland, Yugoslavia and Spain, however, isolated indications of development are evident which one day may play an important part.

Development in Brazil, Venezuela and Mexico has recently made rapid strides, so that Latin America may rank with the U.S.A. and Europe as a center of future architectural development. While Japan has an indigenous architecture of a high standard the representative buildings of Africa, India and Burma are still mostly designed by architects from other countries, who naturally take account of their peculiar local character.

Modern architecture in Canada, Australia and South Africa, the Near East, Argentina and the other South American states is for the present still limited to outstanding isolated achievements and is not in the full sense evidence of a wide-spread new start.

U.S.A.

It is no exaggeration to say that the most decisive happenings in the architectural realm have already shifted from Europe to the New World. This is due to a variety of factors: the fundamental importance of the Chicago School which was first in satisfying the diverse claims of economics, technical science and architecture; the new spatial conception of Frank Lloyd Wright; the educational example of Walter Gropius, Marcel Breuer and Ludwig Mies van der Rohe; the new conception of a dynamic architecture as was realized by younger architects like Matthew Novicki, Eero Saarinen, Hugh Stubbins, Eduardo Catalano and others; and – closely linked to this – the opening-up of new structural possibilities through gifted engineers like Richard Buckminster Fuller, Konrad Wachsmann, Salvadori, Weidlinger and Fred Severud.

Already the most important buildings of the 19th century by H. H. Richardson, McKim, Mead and White had tended towards a specifically American style. American architecture achieved its first peak at Chicago which had to be rebuilt in the shortest possible time after the great fire of 1871: from the demands of this economic necessity resulted important consequences.

The new form of office skyscraper was not only conceived from aesthetic considerations but from a new principle of construction, the structural steel frame. This method of construction has determined a substantial part of the recent architecture since the eighties of last century. The steel frame, which had been used previously in England and France, opened up immediately the unlimited possibilities granted to the height of the building and spatial freedom in the interior through the absence of load bearing walls.

Frank Lloyd Wright, the pupil and collaborator of Louis Sullivan, started by taking the results of the Chicago School as a basis.

His work partly continues that of McKim, Mead and White, but he has achieved a new conception of unity of the outside and inside through an open plan and integration with the landscape. In this he was influenced by Japanese architecture. This new unity transformed the modern house fundamentally. In the early Prairie Houses the pronounced character of Wright's designs is already evident, and each of the subsequent buildings adds a new variant to this extremely subjective form of expression. His most important works, such as the Robie House, "Falling Waters", Taliesin West, as well as later structures based on circular or spiral forms, are standard works of American architecture and show the unlimited scope and imagination of creative design.

Frank Lloyd Wright has passed on new basic conceptions to a whole generation of younger architects and has been of lasting influence on the development of modern architecture. He became the example to many young American architects and to the European avant-garde who saw in him the fulfillment of their own early ideals. To have personal experience of a type of architecture which radiates a spatial fascination is of greater importance than looking at intricate or technically refined details. One can consider from this point of view the works of those architects who received decisive stimulus from Frank Lloyd Wright. They are men like Bruce Goff whose churches and houses in Oklahoma outbid the subjectivist tendencies of Wright's

16

work; or Paul Schweikher with his heavy squat houses, churches and schools, who emphasizes the tension of contrasting materials, especially of stone and wood; or Mario Corbett's churches and houses, some of which point to Bernard Maybeck or Edward L. Barnes' Summer Camp at Fishkill in which he developed structures which in their freedom of spatial interrelation are inconceivable without Frank Lloyd Wright's influence; furthermore some designs for churches by Ralph Rapsom and A. Quincy Jones, as well as the works by Alden B. Dow, McKie and Kamrath and a great number of other architects.

More decisive still than the influence of Frank Lloyd Wright was the impact of those Europeans who came to the United States in the twenties and thirties. First arrivals were Eero Saarinen from Finland and Richard Neutra from Austria, followed later by Walter Gropius, Marcel Breuer, Eric Mendelsohn, Ludwig Mies van der Rohe, Konrad Wachsmann and others. More recently, other architects immigrated from China, Japan, Argentina, Norway, Poland and Italy.

The strongest influence was certainly exercised by the work of Walter Gropius, who is teaching at present at Harvard University. Through his exemplary architectural and educational work at the Bauhaus he created the conditions for a new conception of artistic design. The various realms of creative activity were to be co-ordinated by the architect and each individual form was to be brought into a relationship to surrounding forms and to the whole. Economics, technical science and industry were to be drawn upon in the process of work without allowing any of these spheres to elude the co-ordinating architect. Within a team of young architects (The Architects' Collaborative) Gropius is continuing to work on schools, University buildings, houses and on the large-scale project for the Community Center in Tallahassee, in which he and his young collaborators, supported by the ingenious imagination of the engineers Salvadori and Weidinger, is developing a new form of dynamic architecture.

The closest associate of Walter Gropius, the former student and master at the Bauhaus, Marcel Breuer, now ranks alongside his former teacher and is scarcely surpassed by him in his great influence on other architects. Since his removal to America, Breuer, who like Gropius, previously worked some years in England, built mainly houses. During recent years, however, he has also entered upon larger projects like the school buildings for Vassar College in Poughkeepsie, Hunter College in the Bronx, Sarah Lawrence College in Bronxville and the school in Litchfield. Through his collaboration on the Unesco Building in Paris, the "De Bijenkorf" store in Rotterdam and the U.S. Embassy building at The Hague, Breuer's influence is also reacting on Europe.

The most important achievements of the Gropius and Breuer school are by the architects Paul Rudolph, Hugh Stubbins, John Mac L. Johansen, Ulrich Franzen and King-Lui Wu. Paul Rudolph, after his first buildings in Florida, has done impressive projects such as the U.S. Consulate at Amman, the Center for Dramatic Art at Wellesley College and the airport buildings for Sarasota.

Hugh Stubbins, who was called to Harvard University by Gropius in 1939, made his name first of all by school and domestic buildings, and later especially through his design for the Congress Hall in Berlin and for the U.S. Consulate in Tangier. John Mac L. Johansen, who was born in 1916, deviates even farther from the conventional and experiments in such diverse materials as reinforced concrete, plastic, wood and steel. The Chinese King-Liu Wu and the German Ulrich Franzen have recently achieved notice through their houses.

The followers of the great Ludwig Mies van der Rohe, who came to the United States in 1938 and is teaching at the Illinois Institute of Technology, are to be found all over the world. This vast institute in Chicago, the planning and execution of which were entrusted to Mies van der Rohe after his removal to the United

States, is one of the main works of modern architecture and a source of inspiration to young architects. His sky-scraper flats and other living quarters in Chicago together with his excellent one-family and terrace houses have set the standard for the style of dwelling of our time. The Seagram office block in New York and the design for the Theatre in Mannheim are epoch-making witnesses of his works at a more advanced age. It is indeed no surprise that for many young architects the buildings of Mies van der Rohe are regarded as the last word of the architecture of our time.

The after-effects of Mies van der Rohe's example can be observed in two generations. Saarinen, Johnson and Bunshaft belong to the first generation; Pei, Brownson, Gustavson, Sugden and William Sutherland Becket to the second. Eero Saarinen had the most lasting influence and is today considered as one of the most important architects of the United States. After prolonged collaboration with his father Eliel Saarinen, the brillant Finnish architect and town planner, he designed the General Motors Technical Center near Detroit around an artificial lake, which forms a fascinating and colorful group of buildings of masterly proportions with well elaborated details. His later works create standards for a future architecture, surpassing the vocabulary of Mies van der Rohe, like the Kresge Auditorium for the Massachusetts Institute of Technology in Cambridge with its thin shell-concrete dome supported only on three points, the Center of Culture in Milwaukee and the Hockey Stadium for Yale University in New Haven, which constitutes a brilliant modification of the new concept of the cable roof.

Philip Johnson with his one-family houses symbolizes a modern classicist's approach which with his noble interior designs and refined simplicity of proportions corresponds to the historical forms of this style from Pompeii via the Renaissance to the classic revival around 1800. The third great follower of Mies van der Rohe is Gordon Bunshaft, who is working with Skidmore, Owings and Merrill. His main works within this team are the Lever House and the Manufacturers' Trust Company building in New York as well as large projects for the Air Force Academy in Colorado Springs and the Chase Manhattan Bank in New York.

Harrison and Abramovitz as a team have chiefly made their name through office sky-scrapers. The architects Howe and Lescaze had a lasting influence on the shape of the American sky-scraper. In a similar way Albert Kahn influenced the factory building and Victor Gruen the shopping center. The new conception of a dynamic architecture, which is already evident in the latest works of Gropius (TAC), Saarinen and Stubbins, has been most consistently realized in the works of Mathew Nowicki, who came from Poland and died in an accident in 1950. His main work is the Exhibition Hall in Raleigh which was not finished until after his death. Nowicki with the help of the architect W. H. Deitrick and the Norwegian engineer Fred Severud achieved the new creative approach of the building being conceived from the interior. This idea was applied to the dwelling house by Eduardo Catalano. Using the same approach, Harvard built a music pavilion in Florida, Eero Saarinen the Hockey Stadium in New Haven, Raymond and Rado a restaurant in California and Hugh Stubbins the Congress Hall in Berlin.

The new form of flowing space which is brought about by the cable roof and other dynamic conceptions of space opens up new spheres for discovery by the young architects. More than ever will the engineer's importance be increased for the architect. The structures by Richard Buckminster Fuller, Salvadori and Weidlinger, Konrad Wachsmann and Fred Severud have already in their own way arrived at an architectural form which will be decisive for the future. The principle of the system of construction being made into an aesthetic expression, which Mies van der Rohe demanded, has been given impressive solutions in their buildings.

Of great importance for the architecture of the United States is its influence on industrialization. Solutions of pioneering quality were produced by Eames, Saarinen, as well as by Hamilton and Goody. The American avant-garde architecture has still to confine itself in the main to the realm of one-family houses. This situation is unhealthy, because in most cases the large-scale planning is entrusted to official administrative architects or commercial firms. The great problem of industrialization challenges especially the American architect, if he wishes to maintain his position in public life and not allow himself to be overplayed by building firms and commercial enterprises. It is beyond question that America has realized decisive achievements in modern architecture, but it is equally true that the bulk of all things built is without shape or form. The basic demand of the present time is for large scale planning. Beginnings of this can be found in Rockefeller Center; Boston Back Bay Center; the Channel Heights housing estate at San Pedro by Richard Neutra; the housing units in Chicago by Hilbersheimer and Mies van der Rohe; and the designs for Fort Worth in Texas by Victor Gruen.

MEXICO

Since the second World War, Mexico has witnessed a tremendous cultural development which is especially apparent in its architecture. The new National University is the center of all architectural aspirations of the country. After extensive planning preparations the building was started in 1950. By 1952 the main part of the work was finished. The total costs were 160 million pesos. Pedregal, a volcanic desert south of Mexico City, which was first explored for human habitation by Luis Barragan, was chosen as the site for the University City. This University City consists of the buildings for the various faculties and institutes, a museum, the central library, the administrative building, clubs, recreation and sports centers, workshops, stores, garages and students' dormitories. On an extensive plateau, at 6000 ft. above sea level, measuring 7,000,000 square yards, the various buildings are grouped together in exact order in front of the silhouette of the volcanic mountain range. The only road to Mexico City separates the remaining portions of the University City from the impressive stadium by Pérez Augusto Palancios, which is being used for municipal events as well. The predominantly horizontal appearance of the buildings is contrasted by vertical blocks, the whole composition being accentuated by careful landscaping. Pedestrian pathways and roads for vehicular traffic are kept quite apart from one another. Carlos Lazos, who was responsible for the overall planning, said in this connection: "In the United States or in Europe the University buildings are planned by a building contractor or by two or three architects who, in their turn, employ other architects and contractors. This is a form of professional dependence which we have endeavored to eliminate. The new generation of Mexican architects are seeking professional honor as well as financial reward for their work. The University City was built by 140 architects. Each building was designed by two or three architects forming a group which was entirely responsible for the complete work. More important than the achievement in this case is the fact that the architects of Mexico jointly contributed their talents to the task of building the new University."
The result has not been a uniform style of the Ciudad Universitaria. Each of the 140 architects who participated was free to express his own individuality, although group work was done throughout, not only in designing individual buildings but also in respect to the overall planning, the determination of shape and grouping buildings. Everything contributes to a unified composition which is versatile at the same time.

From the outset it was planned to have Mexican artists participate in the work. The main feature of the University City is the Central Library, by Juan O'Gorman, who showed an architectural and at the same time a painter's approach in its design. For Europeans and North Americans this building, which holds a key-place in the entire composition, appears over-decorated. It can only be correctly interpreted from the angle of Mexican folk art. In other countries the University City was strongly criticized, whereas in Mexico it is regarded as the manifestation of contemporary indigenous culture. It should not be overlooked that here the esprit de corps of an entire nation found an authentic expression. Large scale planning of this kind is extremely rare. Considerable courage was needed to erect, in a relatively poor country, a national university which combines the revolutionary tendencies of recent architecture with the inherited values of tradition.

The most distinguished architect in Mexico is Felix Candela, who immigrated from Spain. His work in the University City is the research laboratory for radiography. His imaginative reinforced concrete structures for factories, commercial buildings and churches continue in the tradition of Freyssinet, Maillart and Nervi, who each expressed a particular idea of form. Candela's experiments aim at opening new structural possibilities to the architecture of the future by a perfection of the methods of using reinforced concrete. His buildings in Mexico City are milestones of this development and furthermore are manifestations of a creative genius among the structural engineers of the present time. The latest works of Candela, especially his shell constructions and his designs of hyperbolic paraboloids, are expressions of the new conception of dynamic architecture and will give fascinating spatial effects of a kind which is rare in European architecture.

The works of other architects, such as the apartment buildings and hotels by Vladimir Kaspé, houses by V. de la Lama and J. Sordo Madaleno, churches by Enrique de la Mora, offices by Ricardo de Robina, as well as the works of the two architects from Germany Max Cetto and Mathias Goeritz with one-family houses and the El Eco Experimental museum in Mexico City respectively, illustrate the supremacy and large-scale character of the new Mexican architecture.

The young generation of Mexican architects was able to take these examples as its immediate basis and especially in the realm of the small house has achieved remarkable results. Enrique Castanedo Tamborrel has built schools and apartment buildings as well as houses of a somewhat rhythmical character. Manuel Rosen is known for his textile factory at Guadalupe and some elegant houses at the Pedregal. In addition, Rosen has done work as an industrial designer and lately his town planning schemes have won recognition. Manuel Teja Oliveros and Juan Becerra Vila are trying to introduce prefabrication into Mexico and have built luxury houses in the Mies van der Rohe tradition. Hector Velasquez Moreno and Ramon Torres Martinez, who collaborated in the Medical Faculty Building of the University City, are using for their apartment buildings and office buildings industrialized building methods which they acquired during their studies in the U.S.A. and France.

Carlos B. Zetina, who was born in 1920, and is now a professor at the university, has built houses and apartment buildings as well as the Club Building of the University City. Salvador Ortega Flores, who is of the same age, is a teacher of architecture and has participated in various buildings of the university. He has built numerous schools and houses. Felipe Salido Torres is the architect of a "Cité d'Habitation" as well as of a factory and various houses. Ignazio Medino Roiz was of considerable influence on Mexican school building and in addition has apartment buildings, office buildings, a factory and houses to his credit.

There is an essential difference between a European or North American architect and his counterpart in

Mexico. The latter is his own building contractor at the same time. Almost continually throughout the year he employs a staff of workmen and supervises the execution of the building process at every stage. The important thing is that he fulfills in its entirety the original task of the architect-builder and that numerous architectural decisions are made as the result of his intimate knowledge of the material and its possibilities of application.

VENEZUELA

As in Mexico, Venezuela's architectural achievements are the result of bold planning of extensive projects. Of special interest is the capital and in particular its University. The country has acquired considerable wealth through the production of oil, and the great cities, such as Caracas and Maracaibo have more than doubled their population during the last five years. Even before the second World War, town planners from other countries, such as José Luis Sert, Maurice Rotival and Bob Moses were called in to deal with the problems arising from population changes. Yet in 1946 Caracas was an inconsequential town with inadequate living accommodation, an insignificant administrative center and unsolved traffic conditions. After the war the center of the town was rebuilt in symmetrical order. This monumental creation is dominated by the Avenida Bolivar, which is 35 yards wide and is underground for part of its length. It forms the key to all other planning work. Conspicuous are the symmetrically placed tall office blocks of the Bolivar Center, which incorporate parking spaces, pedestrian areas and a helicopter landing place. Extensive parking spaces, bus stations, restaurants and shops have been arranged below ground.

The plan for a new university at Caracas originated during World War II. In 1943 an Institute was founded with the specific task of planning and building the University City. The old 18th century university did not fit into the pattern of the city, and the planning of a new one became more and more urgent on account of the constantly increasing population.

The master plan of the new University City is the work of Carlos Raul Villanueva. He and Luis Diamini, the president of the Institute of the University City, had in mind to achieve the greatest possible integration of architecture and the visual arts and at the same time to concentrate in one place the most eminent artistic creations of our time. Thus Villanueva's conception of the master plan was achieved in collaboration with painters, sculptors, mosaic artists and ceramic craftsmen from its earliest stages. The most important Venezuela artists who participated in this project are Vigas, Poleo, Castro, Oramas, Manaure, Barrios, Conarvaez, Navarro and Bogen. In addition some of the European avant-garde were commissioned. They were offered a unique opportunity – Henri Laurens at last was able to erect his mighty sculpture "Amphion" in a grand setting.

Similarly settings were provided for Hans Arp's "Shepherd of the Clouds" and Antoine Pevsner's powerful symbol of triumph. The American sculptor-engineer Alexander Calder designed the ceiling for the Auditorium Maximum. The windows and mosaics are by Fernand Léger. Further works of art are by André Bloc and Victor Vasarely.

The master-plan envisages three prominent areas. The first one is grouped round the main piazza and consists of the museum, the campanile, the University Center and the administrative block. The second area comprises the students' "center of culture" with a covered courtyard, a campus, a reception hall and the Auditorium Maximum. The third area dominated by the University Library building which again is linked directly with a number of lecture halls. In addition there is a small concert hall for chamber music. The building which was the last to be completed is the Faculty for Architecture and Town Planning, an eight-story block with an unusual arrangement of sunblinds and a sharp contrast of solid and pierced walls. A low block with toplights on an irregularly shaped roof is placed in juxtaposition.

Carlos Raul Villanueva, the originator of the whole scheme, once said about the architectural conception of the University City: "The spiritual manifestation of the University as well as of the capital city is borne out in the architectural composition which has the Library and the Auditorium Maximum at its center.

Because of its character and inherent solutions, this center affords grand opportunities for a complete integration of architecture with painting and sculpture and thus for the realization of a 'synthesis of the arts'.

In the realm of the visual arts the necessity of an integration of painting and sculpture with architecture was expressed in the return of the old components, 'color' and three-dimensional composition, resulting in the enrichment of the white body of a building by the formal expressions of the individual arts, given authority by a long process of development.

To restrict oneself entirely to a decorative equilibrium, or to bring painting and sculpture into appropriate order would not be of more value than a museum collection, in this sense of a unification of the arts. The idea of this unity can only be brought to a successful result if painting and sculpture receive architectural justification for their presence from the structural conception and from the function of the space elements which constitute the building."

If one draws comparisons between some of the great town-planning achievements of the post-war years outside Europe, say the University Cities of Mexico City and Caracas as also the town of Chandigarh, one finds similarities as well as decisive differences. Very illuminating is a comparison of the University Cities of Mexico City and Caracas. In Mexico indigenous culture was emancipated, Mexican artists were brought forward and the character of the whole conception was an appeal to the living values of a great past.

In Caracas the achievements of the European and North American avant-garde were consciously taken over, although not divorced from the character of the country and its people. In contrast to numerous educational buildings in North America and Europe, the main object of the most important buildings in Caracas is to screen and reduce the intensity of sunshine and to provide cool and shady zones. The equatorial climate of the country, and the altitude of its capital in a mountain valley 3000 feet above sea-level, demand special architectural solutions which are naturally different from those in other countries.

The main building material in South America is concrete, which is preferred to all alternative materials because of its weight and porosity but also on account of its practically unlimited structural possibilities.

A comparison of the University City of Caracas with the town of Chandigarh, Le Corbusier's later work, proves the great superiority of this European genius. The planning ideas in Caracas could rather be related to Le Corbusier's writings of the nineteen-twenties. It is indeed a remarkable fact that Le Corbusier's ideas have actually been realised in Chandigarh, as his grandiose conceptions are still being dismissed as utopian, especially in Europe.

Having achieved considerable prosperity through its oil and United States investments, Venezuela has provided an example of the realization of town-planning ideas which had been considered impracticable.

One of the most extensive housing projects in Venezuela is the "2nd December" quarter of Caracas, which has been in the process of building for some years. The architect is Villanueva in collaboration with Mijares, Hoffmann and Branco. The owner of this immense housing area is a bank in Caracas.

22

Individual groups of high blocks are spaced at considerable distance from one another and have their own kindergartens, schools, shopping centers, churches, theatres, cinemas, playing fields and community centers. These residential quarters are kept free of traffic and through roads connect them with the center of the town. The number of outstanding buildings in Venezuela is constantly growing. Remarkable houses were built by the architects Guido Bermudes, Carlos Guinard and Moisés Benecerraf. Luxurious hotels and clubs by the architects Tomas José Sanatria and Julian Ferris have sprung up. The design for the Heliocoid shopping center in Caracas is by Jorge Romero Gutierrez. It will incorporate 320 shops as well as exhibition halls, a hotel, a swimming pool, garages and offices. The architects Vegas and Galia have designed exhibition buildings and office blocks. A. P. Pietri has built the famous cable-railway station in Caracas. The most daring project is the design for a museum of modern art by Oscar Niemeyer, in the shape of an inverted pyramid.

BRAZIL

For centuries the culture of Brazil was dictated by Europe. In architecture the official taste of the academies was accepted. The "Semana del Arte" Exhibition at São Paolo in 1922, which was organized by the architects Gregori Warchavchik and Flavio de Carvalho, caused a purifying reaction, and the architecture of Brazil gained contact with the revolutionary endeavors in Europe and the U.S.A. Gregori Warchavchik's own house at Vila Mariana, dating from 1927, proved so convincingly the quality of the new architecture on Brazilian soil that Le Corbusier mentioned it as one of the best examples of modern structural principles used in tropical landscape. The house which is interwoven with its surrounding is the result of climate and geographical considerations.

Two societies from that time onwards in creative competition influenced the development of Brazilian architecture: the "Sociedade Pro Arte Moderne" (SPAM), founded by Warchavchik, and the "Club dos Artistas Modernos" (CAM), run by Flavio de Carvalho. In 1936 Le Corbusier went to Brazil and designed the building for the Ministry of Education at Rio de Janeiro, together with Lucio Costa, Oscar Niemeyer, Jorge Machado Moreira and Alfonso Eduardo Reidy. This design with certain modifications was later executed by the Brazilian architects. The completed building is unique in many respects. Philip Goodwin called it "the most beautiful administrative building of the Western hemisphere". Together with the one-family houses by Gregori Warchavchik and the Brazilian Pavilion at the New York World Exhibition of 1939, this building established the world reputation of Brazilian architecture.

The greatest living representative of Brazilian architecture is Lucio Costa. The sensitive art of achieving complete spatial unity of site, plan and elevation, which is a hall mark of many buildings of the younger generation, is visible in his single-family houses, in the Park Hotel at Nova Friburgo, and especially in the apartment houses in the Eduardo-Guinle Park at Rio de Janeiro. Lucio Costa has participated to a considerable extent in a great many projects. He worked in the beginning with Gregori Warchavchik, later with Oscar Niemeyer and younger colleagues. However, the development was not speeded up by individuals but by a group of architects and artists, who placed the common ideal before personal success. It is one of the creative features of Brazilian architecture that in spite of this, solutions were arrived at which are decidedly individual, and even subjectively sophisticated.

The strongest personality with a highly subjective power of original architectural expression is Oscar Niemeyer. His creative ability transforms an initial whimsical design to finished perfection. His invention of unusual forms makes him frequently start architectural fashions. His most important buildings, especially the ones at Pampulha and Belo Horizonte, are not only decisive highlights of Brazilian architecture but are landmarks of the new architecture in a wider sense.

The third great personality of the new Brazilian architecture is Alfonso Eduardo Reidy, who is at present municipal architect of Rio de Janeiro. His name is chiefly connected with the planning and execution of the Pedregulho projects at Rio de Janeiro. The new way of tackling housing problems has here reached one of its high points. This development incorporates 478 dwellings for government officials in one main block of 5 stories, which follows the contours of a hill in its curvature. At Gavea Reidy was able to execute a second housing scheme of similar shape. Further outstanding works of Reidy are the Museum of Modern Art at Rio de Janeiro, the Experimental College at Asunción in neighbouring Paraguay, the Student's Theatre at Campo Grande and the office block of the Rio Grande do Sul Company at Porto Alegre.

A different personality is Rino Levi, who is renowned through his houses, office buildings and cinemas. His main work is the Central Institute for the Treatment of Cancer at São Paulo. It is a hospital of a new type with a teaching annex, a research center, an infirmary for out-patients and a special section for incurable cases, so placed that one part does not interfere with the others. The clear-cut architectural forms of Levi are essentially different from the organically developed ones of Niemeyer and Reidy.

These are not the only Brazilian architects of world renown. Henrique E. Mindlin has built since 1945 houses, offices and hotels as well as having been successful in competitions. The brothers Roberto (Marcelo, Mauricio and Milton) built the Santos Dumont airport at Rio de Janeiro in 1944. (Milton died in 1953). They created thereby one of the best functioning traffic buildings of recent time. Furthermore, they were pioneers in Brazil in the sphere of apartment buildings, especially through their apartment buildings at Botafogo erected in 1947. Olavo Reding de Campos has built luxurious houses and the bathing pavilion at Indaia. Flavio Amilcar Regis acquired special repute through his administrative buildings and a nursery school at São Paulo. Salvador Candia, Plinio Croce and Roberto Aflalo have built housing developments and tall apartment buildings. Jorge Wilhelm, who was born in 1928, did some town-planning work as well as building houses at São Paulo and the Santa Casa clinical hospital at Jau. Sergio Bernardes is known for his imposing country villas, which have been inspired by North America in their basically cubist conception as well as in the interplay of contrasting materials. Bernardes is an important pioneer in Brazil's slowly starting industrialization of building components. The work of Francisco Bolonha, who was born in 1922, shows similar characteristics. His housing developments and country villas as well as a maternity hospital and a kindergarten school are well known. Special attention must be drawn to his settlement for municipal scavenging workers on Paquéta, because here a form of dwelling, unique in its beauty and economy, was found for the lowest income groups. This project which was finished in 1952, together with the Pedregulho project and the housing estate for industrial workers at Santo André by Carlos Frederico Ferreira, is one of the most important social settlements in Brazil and will be a prototype for the development of this hitherto neglected architectural task.

Carlos Frederico Ferreira has made headway in an economic respect, as his week-end house, built in 1949 in the Friburgo mountains costs about as much as a small motor car.

In the social realm there are noticeable differences in Brazil. So far luxury villas and office blocks are predominant. These two types of buildings are often accompanied by a certain extravagance. The "modern" façade is comparable with the ostentation of the European late 19th Century era. Here, too, is noticeable

24

the enormous damage done by unlimited site speculation, which makes any planning in accordance with new living requirements quite impossible. In one sphere Brazilian architecture has failed like that of most other countries; namely in town-planning which should be the healthy foundation for all future building activity and any new social order. There are a number of magnificent development schemes, among others those of Reidy, Mindlin and the town-planning department of Rio de Janeiro under the direction of José de Olivera Reis. But these schemes on the whole have remained in the planning stage or have been executed with compromise solutions. It is significant that in Brazil too the creative initiative originates from the University town of Rio de Janeiro, which was started under the direction of Jorge Machado Moreira. The entire scheme, of which an excellent institute for child welfare was already finished in 1953, is being developed on an island off Rio de Janeiro.

A further essential step towards a new townscape will be the erection of the new capital of Brazil in the interior of the country. The great competition of 1957 has produced so many fundamentally new solutions that one can look forward to the realization of this grandiose idea. Possibly the young architects of Brazil will be in a position to transform into reality the technical, architectural and social aspirations of the present time – a situation which does not exist in any other place in the world in anything like such favorable conditions.

SCANDINAVIA

The new conception of modern architecture has not remained, in the Scandinavian countries, simply a theoretical formula, but has assimilated the indigenous tradition and arrived at a synthesis which, in the words of Siegfried Giedion, is regional without being provincial. Besides Brazil, whose architecture naturally is based on different conditions, Scandinavia and especially Finland is today a main center of organic architecture, which is characterized by adaptation to the landscape and a wise conformity to social reality.

In Finland the breakthrough to the new conception of modern architecture happened in 1930 through the acceptance of the pioneering ideas of Le Corbusier, Gropius and Mies van der Rohe. Endeavors were, however, latent at an earlier date for a revival of architecture, such as is evident in the early work by Eliel Saarinen, who built the main station in Helsinki from 1905 to 1914, or in the so-called Helsinki School by the workers Lindgren, Sonck and J. S. Siren, who were influenced by Saarinen.

The most important personality after Eliel Saarinen, who emigrated to the United States in 1923, is Alvar Aalto. Already his early works, the Sanatorium at Paimio, the Library in Viipuri as well as a number of factories, are not only buildings which show the influence of Le Corbusier and transfer his creative conception to the North, but they are in the handling of materials and in their imaginative content equal to the works of Le Corbusier. Aalto does not confine himself to taking over certain external features but achieves a revolutionary expression from the fundamental conception. Exemplary achievements are his own house (1936), the Finnish Pavilion at the New York World's Fair of 1939, the students' dormitories of the Technical University at Cambridge, Mass.; and the houses, schools, offices and buildings for sports, especially the community center in Säynätsalo, which were built after his return to Finland.

Besides Alvar Aalto a generation of young architects made the small country a laboratory for new ideas. Aarne Ervi designed the Porthania University in Helsinki, the University Library at Turku, as well as houses and holiday homes, schools and industrial buildings. Viljo Rewell, partly in collaboration with Sipari and Petälä has built apartment houses, schools and office buildings. Kaija and Heikki Siren in their extension to the Finnish National Theatre in Helsinki, in the University Chapel of Otaniemi and in the Concert Hall at Lahti achieved subtle effects in the interplay of wood and glass, brick and steel. Siren and his wife, like Aarne Ervi, have attained important results in the use of prefabricated components, as is evident in the housing estates at Tapiola and the apartment buildings at Otaniemi. Jorma Järvi, Jiro Tukkila, Markus Tavio and Aulis Blomstedt are architects who have likewise made important contributions to the new architecture in Finland. One of the youngest Finnish architects is Osmo Sipari, who was born in 1922. He can already look back on considerable achievements in schools, houses and churches some of which were designed in co-operation with Eerikäinen or Rewell.

Sweden's architecture, like that of Finland, was influenced in its early stages of development by the example of two important architects who brought to Sweden the revolutionary spirit of Le Corbusier and Gropius, at the same time modified in a regional sense: E. Gunnar Asplund and Sven Markelius.

Asplund designed the magnificent Stockholm Exhibition of 1930 which was an abrupt rejection of all eclectic or historical architecture, brought back buildings to their basic geometric forms, and proclaimed the spirit of the new age through daring constructions in steel. The later works of Asplund show the increasingly moderate approach of a modern classicist as is evident from the Town Hall at Gothenburg, the municipal library in Stockholm, his own house near the capital, department stores and university buildings, but above all in the main work of his last years, the forest crematorium on the outskirts of Stockholm.

The early work of Sven Markelius is marked by the Concert Hall at Hälsingborg, which was designed in co-operation with Gustave Lyon and built between 1931 and 1933. Markelius' later work was concentrated on offices, commercial buildings and especially housing and the comprehensive planning of neighborhood units.

One of the most famous examples of large-scale planning in Europe is the suburb of Vällingby, near Stockholm. Sven Markelius was the architect in charge of that project.

Domestic architecture owes essential achievements to the Swedes. They developed and tested the various types of building, the narrow apartment buildings, the point block and the Y-shape or cruciform. Neighborhood units arranged in accordance with most advanced points of view have arisen in the satellite towns of Vällingby, Lidingö and Västertorp near Stockholm. The brothers Ahlsen designed the Årsta Center near Stockholm, which through communal institutions has arrived at an appropriate basis for neighborly intercourse on a cultural level. In the Open Air Housing Development of Malmö and in Gothenburg's suburb of Guldheden, as well as in the project for the Rosta district at Örebro by Backström and Reinius, one can note tendencies indicating future trends.

In other spheres, too, remarkable achievements can be recorded. The concert hall in Gothenburg by Nils Einar Eriksson and the municipal theatre in Malmö by Lallerstedt, Hellden and Lewerentz are in emulation of Sven Markelius. In the building of schools Nils Ahrbom, Helve Zimdahl and Paul Hedquist have distinguished themselves. Exemplary factories have been built by O. Almquist, Ralph Erskine and the architects' department of the Swedish Co-operative Societies, which in other realms too have had a great influence on the development of Swedish architecture. Exhibition buildings were erected by the young architects Magnus Ahlgren and Bertil Zeinitz. For hospital buildings the Southern Hospital in Stockholm by H. Cederström is exemplary. Jaenecke and Samuelson working together have found new solutions to domestic architecture. The new architectural problem of a supermarket has been solved by Ralph Erskine at Luleå in the extreme north of the country.

Architecture in Norway, which had to fight opposition more than the other Scandinavian countries during the last decades, has only in recent years achieved an international standard. This is mainly due to the educational achievement of Arne Korsmo. Notable works of recent Norwegian architecture are those of Christian Norberg-Schulz, Hakon Mjelva and Odd Ostbye, Sverre Fehn and Geir Grung.

Denmark with her mere four million people, of whom one-quarter are concentrated in the capital, plays a considerable rôle in the international field. After the still partly romantic work by J. V. P. Klint, Vilhelm Lauritzen and Hans Hansen, it was mainly the brilliance of Arne Jacobsen which achieved world rank for Danish architecture. He united in a perfect manner the classical Danish tradition with international revolutionary achievements in his works like the House of the Future (1929), a circular house with space for helicopter landings, the housing developments and sports buildings at Bellavista (Copenhagen) and the covered tennis court at Hartmannsvej, the masterly series of town halls at Aarhus, Søllerød and Rødovre, along with schools, factories, flats and offices. The sole preparation for this was the functional architecture of his teacher Kay Fisker. Besides Jacobsen, Arne Lundgren, Eske Kristensen and Mogens Lassen must be mentioned as well as Finn Juhl, who has done mainly interior designs.

The most important personality of the younger generation is Jørn Utzon, born in 1918. When in 1957 he was awarded 1st prize in the international competition for the Sydney Opera House, the architect who up to then was known through his excellent schools and houses stepped right into the center of world news.

It is a fact that his design is a completely personal and fascinating modification of the dynamic architecture which arrived on the scene with Nowicki and Saarinen. Erik Christian Sørensen (born in 1922) built one-family houses which, like Jørn Utzon's house, are in the classical tradition of Mies van der Rohe and are distinguished by sensitive contrasts of materials. The same applies to the houses and school at Gladsaxe by Eva & Nils Koppel. At the same place Knud Hallberg built a housing development which is of interest, especially in the arrangement of the interiors. The series of Denmark's masterly one-family houses is continued with the works of Henrik Iversen and Harald Plum at Holte, Gentofte and Charlottenlund. The young architects Halldor Gunløgsson and Jørn Nielsen have built, apart from houses, the town halls at Kastrup and Fredericia as well as the school at Slagelse.

GREAT BRITAIN

Because of early industrialization Great Britain gained a start over other countries. As early as 1800 the great engineers had obtained practical results with cast iron, the most significant building of the 19th century, the Crystal Palace (1851) by Joseph Paxton, anticipating many of the essentials of modern architecture. A different line of development was started by William Morris and Philip Webb who, unlike Paxton, were inspired by those romantic ideals that had their origins in the Gothic Revival, also by ideals of fine craftsmanship. Towards the end of the century, through the work of the Glasgow school and more particularly of Charles Rennie Mackintosh, Britain also saw the climax of Art Nouveau. The Glasgow Art School (1899) is an outstanding work of its kind. Houses by C. A. Voysey, Norman Shaw, Gimson, Askbee and others, had a profound influence on the Continent, as did the Garden City work of Ebenezer Howard.

More recently the larger cities, and the London area in particular, have seen the building of many housing developments and large apartment buildings. Most of these are purely speculative but many are built by local authorities. An early example of apartment building, in 1933, was Highpoint 1. at Highgate, London, by Tecton – a group of young progressive architects. This was a high point block with central circulation and piloti. Since the war interesting housing has been built at Finsbury by Lubetkin and Skinner (former members of the Tecton group), in which high blocks and low terrace housing are combined. Similar housing has also been designed by, among others, Frederick Gibberd, by Chamberlin, Powell and Bon at Golden Lane, London, and on a large scale by Powell and Moya in Pimlico, London. On the outskirts of London large housing developments of great architectural significance have been designed by the Architect's Department of the London County Council (Chief Architect: Sir Leslie Martin and Robert Matthew, more recently Hubert Bennett). These schemes have low two-story housing, also some excellently designed point blocks (eleven stories which is high for Britain) planned at well-spaced intervals, thus realizing something of Le Corbusier's original Ville Radieuse conception.

Recent school buildings are the culmination of a remarkable story. As early as 1900 experiments were made with classrooms planned to open onto the garden, but the first real break with the courtyard tradition came with the Village College at Impington, Cambridge, designed in 1936 by Walter Gropius and E. Maxwell Fry. After the war the County of Hertfordshire developed this open plan further; it also developed an ingenious system of prefabricated components. This system spread and has been used in schools all over the country by such exponents of modern architecture as Yorke, Rosenberg and Mardall, Cadbury Brown, Clarke Hall, James Cubitt, Richard Sheppard and Peter and Alison Smithson. The latter designed the school at Hunstanton which, in its ruthless detail and uncompromising use of purely functional materials, has become the symbol of "the new brutalism".

In 1951 the Festival of Britain produced a number of exhibition buildings which popularized modern architecture and decor. The largest, though only temporary, was the vast Dome of Discovery – an aluminum dome on delicate supports – by Ralph Tubbs. The Royal Festival Hall, now London's main concert hall, was designed by the Architect's Department of the London County Council. It is brilliantly planned to take advantage of the river side and has a high standard of acoustics. Externally it is more open to criticism.

While church buildings remain almost entirely within traditional forms or try to mingle these with modern elements, hospitals, hotels and community centers have shown better results: for example, the hospital at Londonderry by Yorke, Rosenberg & Mardall; the Y. M. C. A. Hostel for Indian students in London by Ralph Tubbs; the Community Centre at St. Olave's, Suffolk, by Tayler; the hospital at Wallingford, Berkshire, by Powell & Moya, as well as the same architects' extensions to the Fairmile Hospital; the Y. M. C. A. Hostel at Portsmouth by F. J. Guy; the Motel at Dover by Louis Erdi, and the Community Centre at Doncaster by Frederick Gibberd.

Offices and commercial buildings have remained of little importance to the development of modern architecture in Great Britain. In contrast, designs for factories were early distinguished by their functional order and daring approach to building. Outstanding individual achievements were the chemical factories at Beeston by Sir Owen Williams, built in 1930/32 and famous for their uncompromising use of reinforced concrete and glass. Further important factories are those near Manchester by Taylor, Young and Matthew; at Dagenham by Edward D. Mills; at Wallsend-on-Tyne by S. W. Milburn; at Debden by Easton and Robertson; in Hemel Hempstead by Ove Arup and at Gateshead, County Durham, by Yorke, Rosenberg and Mardall.

Among the traffic and exhibition buildings London's underground stations must be mentioned; the air terminal at Edinburgh by Robert Matthew and the hangars at Filton near Bristol by Eric Ross. The design by James Dartford for an aerodrome at an extreme height above London supported by three lift-shafts as well as the design by Clive Entwistle for a new Crystal Palace (1946) constitute visions projected into the distant future.

The situation as a whole is at present strongly influenced by a traditional outlook. Structural masterpieces like the famous Penguin Pool in the Regents Park Zoo by Lubetkin & Skinner have remained individual solutions which did not assert any influence on the situation as a whole. The main emphasis apart from the building of schools is directed to the building of housing estates which are more and more arranged as large-scale town planning schemes.

The latest works by Powell & Moya, some of the satellite towns near London, and especially the prolific activity of the London County Council, indicate positive tendencies of future development.

THE NETHERLANDS

The actual beginning of recent Dutch architecture can be traced back to one important building, the Amsterdam Stock Exchange by Hendrik Petrus Berlage, which was finished as early as 1898. In the various preliminary designs for this building Berlage's pioneering architectural gift is manifested. Starting with a traditional conception influenced by Cuypers, he developed into a new evaluation of local materials and their appropriate application.

The succeeding development at first passes through a phase of extreme negation of Berlage's principles and achieves fascinating results through romanticizing experiments with materials as evident in the buildings of the Amsterdam School. The apartment buildings by M. de Klerk built in the twenties and thirties of this century are outstanding for their fantastic articulation of wall surfaces and expressive handling of volumes. But, in spite of this, a progressively increasing simplification and abstraction of the individual blocks can be observed.

The influence of Frank Lloyd Wright, who had been encouraging European architects in their aims since 1910, has been particularly evident here.

The conception of the new style is based upon the works of the great painters and sculptors, who since the birth of cubism stood for a completely fresh approach towards works of art. The Dutchman Piet Mondrian became, through his neoplastic pictures and theories, of decisive importance for architecture. In 1917 architects Oud, Rietveld and van Eesteren formed the De Stijl group together with the painters Mondrian and van Doesburg as well as the sculptor Vantongerloo. Centrally controlled town planning was achieved through C. van Eesteren.

In the building of apartments and housing developments new types were evolved which remained models also for international development. J. J. P. Oud has been building housing projects since 1919 in Rotterdam and the Hook of Holland. They are self sufficient neighborhoods built under such stringent financial conditions as have seldom been equalled since. W. van Tijden and Maaskant as well as Brinkman and van der Vlugt developed new forms of high apartment buildings in imposing groupings in Rotterdam. G. Rietveld in his house at Utrecht combined all recently discovered individual results in one building of superb spatial harmony.

Other building tasks too were fundamentally transformed. In particular schools afford outstanding examples of the change in the attitude to building. The masterly school buildings of Willem M. Dudok at Hilversum bring out a quiet harmony of horizontal and vertical surfaces. Duiker and Bijvoet created different pedagogic presumptions in the Amsterdam open air school and van der Vlugt in the Crafts School at Groningen. Commercial and factory buildings were given expressions suited to the present in accordance with the law of the new architecture that function of the building must play a part in fashioning its external appearance. The famous Van Nelle factory by Brinkman and van der Vlugt, finished in 1930, must be mentioned as being in the front rank. The building is totally encased in glass and by having the supports set back affords an independent positioning of departments in accordance with the demands of the business.

An outstanding early example of the building of department stores was the "Bijenkorf" in Rotterdam by Willem M. Dudok, erected in 1930. The clear emphasis of the horizontal, and the masterly proportions of glass and walls have made it one of the most important modern buildings of its kind. It was destroyed during the war but was rebuilt by Breuer, Elzas and Schwarzman. It became a feature of the central shopping area of Rotterdam through its appearance adapted to the altered conditions of the age as well as through the incorporation of important works of art. The best known group of buildings featuring Dutch post-war architecture is the "Lijnbaan" shopping center in Rotterdam, by J. H. van den Broek and J. B. Bakema. It offers a completely new conception of this type of building by providing a shopping street consisting of small individual shops flanking a pedestrian zone. In its general lay-out Rotterdam is an outstanding example of the rebuilding of a city center. Van den Broek and Bakema with their high apartment houses have played a considerable part therein. Other outstanding apartment houses were built at Schiedam by E. F. Grossman.

The great tradition of Dutch architecture in the twenties and thirties could not be continued on the same level in more recent times. There is a comparatively high architectural level and numerous buildings still bear witness to a remarkably cultured way of life. One cannot help noticing, however, that the lofty pioneering spirit of the twenties has given way to a moderate and sometimes stagnating attitude. The pioneers no longer point the way to the future. J. J. P. Oud has designed other remarkable school buildings, and the sculpture pavilion at Arnhem by G. Rietveld may even usher in new tendencies in the realm of museum buildings, but these achievements are not carried through by a new generation. The latest architects of Holland like Penning, Warners, Konynenburg, Haan and van Eyck are trying, for the time being, to base their work on international achievements and are forming the basis in their own country for the tasks of the future which the new social pattern will demand.

BELGIUM

In the first stages of the development of modern architecture, Belgium, like Holland, has contributed more than most of the other European countries. While the Netherlands had their prime in the first three decades of this century, Belgium's architectural prime was during the last decade of the 19th century. Brussels at that time was the center of the European cultural movement in addition to, and at times even more so than Paris. Brussels provided the first positive reception of the decisive works of the great pioneers in painting, sculpture, literature and architecture. In Victor Horta and Henry van de Velde the little country had personalities who were of significance for future architectural development in Europe. Horta confined his activity in the main to Brussels, where he built apartment houses and communal buildings with iron and glass, both newly discovered materials so far as architecture is concerned. These buildings demand to be recognized as the most mature examples of the Jugendstil. More than any other architect of this movement he was able to give architectural expression to the dynamic force of the line and at the same time to open up new and future possibilities for the use of iron. Henry van de Velde, who laid the foundation of the theory of the Jugendstil, at that time had only a few buildings in Belgium to his credit, and made his real impact through his work in Germany. Such buildings as the Hohenhof in Hagen (Westphalia) and the Werkbund Theatre in Cologne are perfect examples of a plastic handling of structure and detail. His interior designs became symbols of a new way of living.

Besides Horta and van de Velde, Victor Bourgeois is the third great personality of recent Belgian architecture. His "Cité Moderne" in Brussels, which he built between 1921–22 as a comprehensive housing development, represents one of the earliest solutions of such a task.

While Horta and van de Velde made a considerable impact on European development, architecture in Belgium itself, with few exceptions, has remained restricted to traditional academic and eclectic representational buildings. Only quite recently new ways are becoming evident which may lead to a healthier state of architectural environment. In Antwerp new housing developments have been built by the architects Maes, Maeremans and Braem. In Liège the Egau Group was responsible for a number of high apartment houses which are modelled on the main achievements in other countries. Furthermore the young architects Constantin L. Brodzki, Henri Montois and Robert Courtois are outstanding with their small houses and apartment buildings as well as exhibition and commercial buildings. Possibly the Brussels World Exhibition of 1958 will give a new impetus to Belgian architecture.

GERMANY

In Germany the conception of modern architecture, similar to that of nearly all previous periods, was taken up from the countries of origin at a relatively late date, but then consistently developed to the full. Essential ideas were adopted from Great Britain, France, Belgium and the United States, and then further developed. The most important buildings, crucial for future development, were the Wertheim department store in Berlin by Alfred Messel; the Hohenhof at Hagen by Henry van de Velde, the buildings of Heinrich Tessenow at Dresden-Hellerau, the Hochzeits-Turm in Darmstadt by J. M. Olbrich, the AFG Turbine Hall in Berlin by Peter Behrens, the Chemical Factory in Luban by Hans Poelzig and the Centenary Hall in Breslau by Max

Berg. Of essential influence became the co-operation of creative architects and artists with manufacturers and business men in the German Werkbund, founded in 1907, which became of importance for international development. Starting from this basis new lines of development lead to the buildings by Walter Gropius, who already before World War I through the factory in Alfeld near Hanover and the one at the Werkbund Exhibition in Cologne brought about a new outlook on the use of materials. Further exponents of that line were Ludwig Mies van der Rohe, whose Weissenhof-Siedlung, a housing project near Stuttgart, combined the efforts of the most important architects of the avant-garde like Adolf Rading, Ernst May, Eric Mendelssohn, Bruno and Max Taut, Hans and Wassili Luckhardt, Heinz and Bodo Rasch, as well as a great number of other architects. The Bauhaus, founded in Weimar and later removed to Dessau, combined the individual lines of development of the international avant-garde and laid the foundations for fresh architectural education in the world. Designed by Gropius, the school and its ancillary buildings for the teaching staff are leading works of the New Architecture. At the same time, and sometimes in opposition to the endeavors of the Bauhaus, Hugo Häring and Hans Scharoun developed new forms of organic design, which enriched German architecture just as did the buildings by Hans Poelzig, Wilhelm Kreis and Fritz Höger, as well as the church builders Otto Bartning, Dominikus Böhm and Rudolf Schwarz. The whole range of building tasks from the agricultural, factory, office, school and community building to the housing development and town planning were brought towards their appropriate solution. This very promising development ended with the political changes of 1933. The Bauhaus was shut down in 1932 and many of the best architects emigrated to other countries. With the exception of a few industrial buildings and works related to traffic problems, architecture stagnated in pseudo-monumental representation and a misunderstood classic revival.

After the collapse of National Socialism attempts were at first made to link architecture as well as other things to the days prior to 1933. The task was not only to overcome the dictator's style, but over and above that architects were forced through fundamentally changed architectural conceptions to find solutions for the creation of a new environment. In the beginning only a few cities decided on sweeping measures; thus Hanover through Hillebrechts' initiative, then Kiel and Cologne. In more recent times the Hanseatic cities, notably Hamburg and Bremen arrived at large-scale town planning schemes. Town planning is the foundation for all other tasks, which by ignoring town-planning laws lose their own value even where artistic maturity of the highest order is evident. This is of particular importance in respect to residential buildings. By 1945 about 25% of the total dwellings were destroyed. While the emergency buildings of the first post-war years were put up without planning and with insufficient material, the situation has improved since 1950. A housing project comprising solely of high apartment houses was built at the Grindelberg in Hamburg between 1950 and 1956. A mixed development of high and low buildings was erected in the housing developments at Cologne, Munich, Leverkusen (near Cologne), Frankfurt, Bad Godesberg, Hanover and Bremen. A further example was provided by the International Building Exhibition in Berlin in 1957, for which the old Hansa Quarter was rebuilt by numerous German and foreign architects.

In the realm of office and administrative buildings private enterprise has made new architectural solutions possible, but they are swamped by the mass of cliché buildings. Exceptions are the works of Friedrich Wilhelm Krämer at Brunswick and Heilbronn; of Hermann Wunderlich in Cologne; Paul Schneider Esleben in Düsseldorf and Otto Apel in Frankfurt-on-Main.

Of the new theatre buildings the Municipal Theatre at Münster (Westphalia) must be mentioned; it was completed by Deilmann, von Hausen, Rave and Ruhman in 1956. In spite of difficult conditions it became an imposing building with a fine auditorium. The designs of Ludwig Mies van der Rohe for the Mannheim National Theatre and of Hans Scharoun and Hermann Mattern for the State Theatre in Kassel have unfortunately remained projects only. At Mannheim the building was executed by Gerhard Weber, but nevertheless it is one of the most beautiful buildings of post-war German architecture. Of the German concert halls, besides the great broadcasting studio of the Hessian Radio by Gerhard Weber, the concert hall of the Berlin Academy for Music by Paul Baumgarten should be mentioned; it was finished in 1954.

Schools and youth hostels are distinguished by remarkable quality in Germany, although important influences from Northern Europe and from America cannot be ignored. Besides the buildings for the University of Frankfurt-on-Main by Ferdinand Kramer and the Technical High School in Darmstadt, a striking example of German university architecture is the High School of Design at Ulm by Max Bill, which also from the pedagogic angle attempts a new approach in conjunction with the Bauhaus ideas. The school buildings of recent years, especially those by Wilhelm, Seitz and Krämer, correspond in an exemplary way to the demands of a new pedagogical conception. A particularly fine example of the new youth hostels is the one by Hubert Hoffmann on the Venusberg near Bonn.

Among hospital buildings first of all the ones in Marl (Westphalia) by Werner Hebebrand and Walter Schlempp must be mentioned, as well as the designs for the surgical clinic at Düsseldorf by Gustav Hassenpflug and the sanatorium in Bad Salzuflen by Harald Deilmann, erections of several wings leading to a fresh differentiation of the various functions of this building task. The rebuilding of churches is especially concentrated in Germany in areas such as North Rhine/Westphalia and Franconia.

Exhibition buildings are in every way comparable with those of other countries. Soon after the war they were already of a high standard. The Berlin City Pavilion by Eduard Ludwig at the German Traffic Exhibition in Munich and the one for the Constructa in Hanover by Hans & Wassili Luckhardt have become works of art created with the aid of rationalized methods of construction. Outstanding results of architecture achieved with the means of our time are the buildings of Bernhard Hermkes in Hamburg such as the Philipsturm and the Plant Exhibition House, as also the Exhibition Restaurant of the Federal Garden Show of 1953 in Kassel by Hermann Mattern, and more recently the structures of the young Berlin engineers Frei Otto and Günter Günschel.

The demands of modern traffic cannot be avoided much longer by German architecture. In addition to new roads and bridges, underpasses and raised crossings, more petrol stations and multi-level garages must be built. Lothar Götz has done exemplary work with his petrol stations near Frankfurt-on-Main. The multi-level garage, which has been successful for a considerable time in North America and Italy was introduced into Germany by Paul Schneider-Esleben with his garage at Düsseldorf in 1952–53.

The most advanced section of German post-war architecture is factory design. The weaving works at Blumberg by Egon Eiermann, which has attracted considerable attention in other countries, has not been surpassed in Germany. Other works by Egon Eiermann as well as by Paul Schneider-Esleben, Friedrich Wilhelm Krämer and Fritz Schupp show the high quality of industrial building.

SWITZERLAND AND AUSTRIA

Austria and Switzerland have gone different ways in their architectural development. While Austria was a pioneering country around 1900 yet later fell back, the contribution of Switzerland came relatively later, but has remained remarkable up to the present time. Both countries have a tendency towards the conservative which is inherent in domestic tradition.

Of outstanding importance for recent architecture was Otto Wagner, who saw structure, material and style in a new relationship based on the theory of Gottfried Semper. His buildings for the Vienna city railway and the Post Office Savings Bank are main works of modern architectural development, which showed as early as 1905 the artistic possibilities of iron and glass as new materials in design.

His pupil and associate of later years Josef Hoffmann was able to start from the ideas of his teacher. His many various exhibition buildings, interior designs and the famous Palais Stoclet in Brussels fascinate through their rectangular simplifications and strong contrasts of black and white. The later works of Hoffmann had decisive influence on social housing construction. The third great Austrian pioneer, Adolf Loos, is about the same age as Hoffmann. The complete abolition of ornamentation in architecture and applied art was the object of his uncompromising fight. He aimed at achieving aesthetic effect solely through the clear articulation of well-proportioned building components. His epoch-making buildings like the house on the Michaeler-Platz in Vienna from 1910 or the various and sometimes earlier villas are significant forerunners of contemporary architecture through the simplicity of their structure.

These great pioneers, to whom one can add Josef Maria Olbricht with the Vienna Secession Building of 1898–99 and in more recent times Josef Frank with important apartment buildings, had really no successors of equal weight. Peter Behrens' teaching at the Vienna Academy from 1922 to 1936 remained without actual effect in Austria.

The architects of the present time are therefore not able to follow a tradition but are forced to model themselves on foreign examples. Besides the buildings by Clemens Holzmeister in Vienna and Linz, and by Franz Schuster in Vienna and Darmstadt, special mention must be made of the work by Roland Rainer and Carl Auböck, who have made very interesting experiments in the realm of prefabricated housing.

The new architecture in Switzerland is essentially conservative and only at a late date accepted and assimilated the achievements of neighboring countries. An exception is the work of Robert Maillart, who is by far the most important exponent of modern architectural development in Switzerland. The ingenious bridges in isolated valleys, his early mushroom constructions as well as the inimitable parabolic shell at the National Exhibition in Zürich are highlights of modern design forms and without comparison in Switzerland. About 1930 young Swiss architects joined forces for the erection of the "Neubühl" Werkbundsiedlung, a housing project in Zürich. They were M. E. Haefeli, Carl Hubacher, Rudolf Steiger, Werner M. Moser, Emil Roth, Paul Artaria and Hans Schmidt. Previously and later on they were known for representative buildings designed by them as individual architects. This housing project in the south of Zürich, comprising about 200 living units, was to Switzerland a demonstration of the new architecture. Other housing projects were patterned more strongly on indigenous tradition. The Wädenswil settlement by Hans Fischli and O. Stork must be mentioned, furthermore the housing development in Basle by Hermann Baur, which comprised a community center, an open-air swimming pool, a pavilion school and a water-tower in its lay-out. New pioneering designs for complete residential neighborhoods were produced by Niklaus Morgenthaler in collaboration with "Atelier 5". The block of one room apartments in Basle by Artaria and Schmidt is unthinkable without Le Corbusier. The two apartment buildings in Zürich built by Marcel Breuer and Alfred and Emil Roth in 1935–36 for Siegfried Giedion show, in spite of close conformity with international development, clear signs of design forms which are specifically Swiss. There are further noteworthy houses by Max Bill in Zürich, by Otto & Walter Sann near Herzensee, by Hans Brechbühler in Bümplitz and by Albert F. Zeyer in Lucerne. It goes without saying that Le Corbusier's house at Ouchy on the Lake of Geneva, which was built in 1923–24 in spite of many obstacles, is the most outstanding building of this series and the unequalled standard for many architects. Only quite recently the attempt has been made to create new types of one-family houses. Thus Justus Dahinden is basing his design on the prismatic structure of a pyramid, Wolfgang Behles, Leo Hafner and Alfons Wiederkehr are arriving at more freely shaped plans and unevenly pitched or butterfly roofs reminiscent of Italian examples. Thomas Schmid in the clear cubistic forms of his houses has reflected his experiences gathered in the United States. In the sphere of point blocks Helfer, Somazzi and Wirz are pioneers with their buildings in Berne.

Switzerland shows a high standard in her school buildings, especially of primary schools which are often combined with kindergarten establishments. Here first mention may be made of the school in the Bruderholz in Basle by Hermann Baur, which is freely integrated with the landscape through its system of pavilions. Other schools by A. H. Steiner, Emil Jauch, Erwin Bürgi and E. Gisel show the transformed character of the new school buildings which is now opened to light and air and is adapted to the new teaching methods.

Compared with the clarity and economy of the new school buildings Swiss universities in general afford relics of the representational manner of building. The Arts and Crafts school in Berne by Hans Brechbühler can so far be regarded as one of the main achievements of Swiss architecture. The Cantonal Library at Lugano by Carlo and Rino Tami is strongly influenced by the new Italian spirit in its spatial order and outward appearance and also indicates Switzerland's cultural link with the South.

Extreme care for the healthy development of the child is not only evident in school buildings but even more so in kindergarten and sports grounds. The very early kindergartens at Winterthur include those by Reinhart, Ninck and Landolt, at Davos-Platz by Rudolf Gabarel and at Glarus by Hans Leuzinger. Later examples are by Henry Daxelhofer and Karl Müller, Josef Schütz, Alfred Roth and Franz Scheibler.

Church building in Switzerland has been stimulated above all by the work of Herman Baur and Karl Moser. The Antonius Church in Basle by Karl Moser was built in the middle twenties and is among the first churches to show exposed reinforced concrete. The later church buildings by Werner Moser, Fritz Metzger, Karl Egender, Hans Hofmann and A. H. Steiner cannot stand comparison with the early examples.

The National Exhibition at Zürich in 1939 marks the beginning of a number of contemporary exhibition buildings. Hans Hofmann designed the Great Hall, which consisted of a steel structure covered with canvas, and incorporated areas at the sides for extending the capacity of the hall when occasion demanded. The Flower Hall by Werner Krebs was of simple timber and glass construction. In the same year the "Tonhalle" by Haefeli, Moser and Steiger, was built in Zürich and became the most important concert hall in Switzerland. A significant contribution to theatre building was achieved in the Park Theatre at Grenchen by Ernst Gisel. Of the large sports grounds in Switzerland, the covered stadium at Oerlikon (Zürich) by Karl Egender and the swimming pools by Piccard in Lausanne, by Frey and Schindler in Olten, by Haefeli and Moser in Zürich, by M. Rasser and T. Vadi in Basle and by Max Frisch in Zürich must be mentioned.

Offices and factory buildings were for a long time considered a field of no importance in Switzerland. Great progress in breaking this prejudice was made by O. R. Salvisberg's buildings in Zürich and Basle as well as by the offices and boiler-house at Arbon by Dubois and Eschenmoser. The power station at Töss (Winterthur) by the brothers Pfister was built in 1925. It is a simple hall structure with continuous rough plan fenestration. The General Motors factory of 1935 in Biel by R. Steiger and C. Hubacher, comprised an assembly shop, power station and offices with roof garden and exhibition space. Present-day examples are the power station at Birsfelden by Hans Hofmann, the factory at Horgen (Zürich) by Hans Fischli; the factory at Gossau by Danzeisen; the watch-making factory at Lengnau by Max Schlup and the winter-quarters for a circus at Rapperswil by Wolfgang Behles, born in 1929.

ITALY

Italian twentieth century architecture arrived late on the scene of international development. After the buildings in the Jugendstil by Raimondo d'Aronco and Ernesto Basila, which were in part influenced by Viennese architects, the great hopes of Italian architecture were Antonio Sant'Elia and the sculptor Umberto Boccioni. They were both victims of World War I. Sant'Elia was one of the most important personalities of the Futurist movement, which through the early death of these two leading masters lost its creative energy. When Antonio Sant'Elia died at the age of 28 none of his brilliant designs had been executed. His ideas and a few projects, however, determined the picture of recent Italian architecture. In 1914 Sant'Elia in a manifesto on the occasion of an exhibition of his town planning schemes wrote:
"We have to find new forms, a new harmony of the solids, an architecture whose justification for existence can only be sought in the special conditions of modern life... we have lost the sense for the monumental, for the heavy, the static... we have enriched our realm of perception with the taste for the airy, the practical, the ephemeral, the speedy... We have to invent and build a city, a futurist city, which is quick, movable and dynamic in all its components. I maintain that futurist architecture must be an architecture of reinforced concrete, of glass, of iron, of plastics and of those substitutes for wood, stone and brick, which alone guarantee a maximum of elasticity and lightness. I maintain that decoration as a component foreign to architecture is an absurdity... only through the use of the untreated materials will result the decorative value of futurist architecture..."
After World War I an academic neo-classicism spread in Italy which met the petit bourgeois' ambitions of the dictatorial regime. The façades of M. Piacentini from then onwards for some decades stood in un-compromising contradiction to the new movement of rationalism. In scarcely any country was the lining up in opposite camps between the mediocre and the revolutionary endeavors so apparent as in Italy.
In 1927 a number of young architects formed a group under the name of "Group 7". This was uncompro-misingly directed against the "official" architecture, and sought to establish a link with architectural development in Northern Europe, which was far ahead of Italy in its theoretical work on new aims as well as in the realization of individual buildings. The group consisted of the Milan architects Figini, Frette, Larco, Pollini, Rava, Terragni and Castagnoli but soon after its formation the Roman architects Libera and Trucco joined it.
The intellectual head of this movement was Giuseppe Terragni who created the most convincing buildings incorporating in the greatest purity the spirit of the New Architecture, as in his schools, houses, an orphanage and the Fascist Party House in Como. In spite of the occasional sharp attacks on Group 7, at the

beginning pioneering buildings were still possible under the Fascist regime. Only through the influence of National Socialism did neo-classical pseudo-architecture finally gain the ascendancy.

Essential stages in the development of rationalist architecture in Italy in the twenties and thirties are the Fiat Car Factory in Turin by Matté Trucco (1927), buildings at the Milan Triennale of 1933 by Aloisio and Chessa as well as those by the team of Portaluppi, Banfi, Belgioso, Peresutti and Rogers, the Tuberculosis Examination Center at Alessandria by Ignazio Gardella (1935 to 1938) as well as Sant'Elia Kindergarten and a number of villas and apartment houses in Como by Giuseppe Terragni. One must add the outstanding works of Pier Luigi Nervi, like the Stadium in Florence, built in 1932, and the hangars near Orbetello (1938).

The new architecture in Italy only achieved wider influence after the downfall of the Fascist dictatorship. Only then were the so far latent formal qualities brought to full development and architecture imbued with imaginative audacity and artistic diversity, which in the rest of Europe is only slowly developing. An architecture developed whose national idiom is expressed in delight in spatial and color experiments as in the integration with painting and sculpture.

The main problem of architecture in Italy, as in many other countries, was housing. The shortage of dwellings was not only a consequence of the war; it already existed through the ever-increasing population and was only aggravated manifold by war damage. It came to a serious crisis in the years 1940 to 1945. More than six million dwellings had been destroyed. After 1945 an extensive building program was started, mainly promoted by the State. The so-called INA House Plan envisaged the erection of 180,000 dwellings over a period of seven years with the minimum of financial means. Apart from this, impressive apartment houses in large towns, three-story blocks of apartments and luxurious private homes with designs conditioned by climate and their position in the urban or rural scene were built by Ugo and Amedeo Luccichenti, Vincenzo Monaco, Paolo Chessa, Pietro Lingeri, Luciano Galmozzi, Melchiorre Bega, Ico and Luisa Parisi, Julio Lafuente and Luigi Moretti.

Figini and Pollini have built outstanding housing projects for the firm of Olivetti. A. Libera, Victorio Gandolfi, Carlo Luigi Daneri and Mario Fiorentino created compact residential districts in Genoa, Milan and Rome. Guiseppe Samona designed Venice's satellite town of Ozelin.

Italian architecture is distinguished by its exhibition buildings and railway stations. The most famous example is the Termini Station in Rome, completed in 1950 by Calini, Castellazzi, Fadigati, Montuori, Pintonello and Vitellozzi working as a team. The magnificent transparency of its horizontally emphasized façade with the glass-clad entrance and the excellent orderliness of the traffic arrangement have made this building the most modern railway station in Europe. The design for the Naples station by Castiglioni, Bongioanni and Sianesi suggests a dynamic structure whose elements are simultaneously part of a new large scale ornamentation.

A work of classical simplicity and extraordinary audacity of vaulting is the Flower Hall at Pescia by Enzo and Giuseppe Gori, Leonardo Ricci, Leonardo Savioli and the engineer Emilio Brizzi. The Fishmarket Hall at Ancona by Gaetano Minuccio is also worthy of mention. Brilliant designs were effected by Gio Ponti who, like many other Italian architects, works as an industrial designer as well. His designs for the Pirelli skyscraper and for buildings in South America and Sweden have caused a world-wide stir.

Among the buildings for cultural and social purposes the museums by Albini and Gardella, the children's town in Trieste by Marcello d'Olivo, the Park Library in Milan by Ico & Luisa Parisi and the sport center in Salsomaggiore by V. Vigano are outstanding. Churches in their order of importance are far behind other building tasks. Factories which reflect the new spirit are by Figini and Pollini, Luigi Cosenza, Eduardo Vittoria and Giorgio Baroni who have developed new structural ideas.

FRANCE

France along with Great Britain has been the main stimulator in the development of modern architecture. The brilliant engineering works by Labrouste, Contamin and Eiffel were already realizations of a new architecture. Building tasks which were the result of the changing times, such as market halls, railway stations, exhibition buildings and department stores in Paris, were great events of the art of engineering undisturbed by the official architectural routine. They laid the foundation for a new manner of building which through its particular principle of construction influenced architecture as a whole. Since the end of the 19th century concrete, in addition to iron, became essential in the further development of French architecture. After the early experiments of the gardener Monnier, François Hennebique discovered the laws inherent in the new synthetic material and applied them to architectural use. The actual conclusions of these laws were drawn by the architects Auguste Perret, Tony Garnier and the brilliant engineer Eugene Freyssinet.

At the beginning of the 20th century Auguste Perret was the dominating figure of French architecture. His works have been exemplary from his early ones in Paris, like the apartment houses in the Rue Franklin, the garage in the Rue Ponthieu of 1905, the dock buildings at Casablanca, the churches at Le Raincy and Montmagny down to numerous houses which were partly designed in collaboration with his brothers Gustave and Claude. These buildings are pioneering solutions through the clarity of their materials and the uncompromising purity of structure.

Tony Garnier designed his "Cité Industrielle" from 1901 onwards. This design brilliantly incorporated the essential tendencies which later became decisive in 20th century development. This plan showed a geometric form with flat roofs, spacious squares and sound traffic arrangements. Garnier was only able to see a fraction of his designs put into practice in Lyon with the stadium, the abattoir, the Grange-Blanche Hospital as well as a number of living quarters.

If we can consider Perret and Garnier as having revived neo-classicism, the work of Freyssinet is emphatically anti-classic. He is completely of the modern functionalist persuasion and in his Zeppelin hangars at Orly created masterpieces of a new architectural dynamic, of a design almost vibrating with inner tension. The determining influence not only for French but for the whole international sphere of architecture was to be the native of Western Switzerland, Le Corbusier. It remained for him to draw the conclusions from the results which Perret and Garnier had discovered through concrete. At the same time he succeeded in using these conclusions in propounding a universally acceptable philosophy of art in close relationship to the social demands. In 1915 Le Corbusier in his model for the houses of the Domino Estate found a fundamental idea, the recurrence of which can be traced in most of his later works; it is the reinforced concrete framework reduced to the simplest formula, allowing every possible freedom to the architect in the arrangement of rooms and partitions. For Le Corbusier the first concern in the twenties was designing the new living unit, whose formula he recast, starting from the design of furniture for the individual room down to most comprehensive plans for housing projects and towns. Landmarks of this endeavor and at the same time landmarks of the international development of architecture are the superb villas at Garches, Auteuil, Boulogne/Seine and Stuttgart as well as the masterpiece in this series, the Villa Savoye at Poissy; furthermore the Pessac housing project near Bordeaux, the Voisin Plan and other projects for towns in France and abroad. About 1930 Le Corbusier turned his attention to more sizeable tasks. The shelter for the homeless, the Swiss Students' Hostel of the University City in Paris as well as the House of the Centrosoyus in Moscow date from that period. The two largest projects of that time, the Palace for the League of Nations in Geneva and the Soviet Palace in Moscow, were victims of the resistance of the ever-increasing reactionary forces. The grandiose plans for a self-sufficient Unité d'Habitation could for the first time be put into practice in Marseilles. They were repeated with modifications at Nantes, in the neighborhood of Paris and in Berlin: The crown of all Le Corbusier's creative efforts is, without doubt, the building of the town of Chandigarh (Punjab), which gave him for the first time the opportunity to realize his vision of a new city. Besides the latter he built the museum and one-family houses in Ahmedabad, the La Tourette monastery, the church near Ronchamp and the Philips Pavilion at the Brussels World Exhibition. Of all these works Ronchamp and the Philips Pavilion give expression to a new concept of dynamic tension in the plastic composition of a building.

The only solution to France's catastrophic housing problem worthy of any promise for the future was offered by Eugène Beaudouin and Marcel Lods with the Cité de la Muette near Drancy in 1933, which was a housing project consisting of a stepped layout of high and low buildings. Only in the most recent time have experiments been undertaken afresh in order to arrive at new solutions in the field of housing. One must mention the buildings by Ginsberg, B. H. Zehrfuss, Alfred L. Henry, Lionel Mirabaud, Jean Nielly, Margaret Tallet, André Wogenscky, Jean Sebag, Henry Pottier and Henry Duverdier. Housing developments were also built by Badani & Roux Dorlut at Villiers-le-Bel, by Candilis and others at Bagnol-sur-Cèze, by Pierre Vago in Le Mans, and by Le Caisne, Rouquet & Pomarède in Villeneuve-le-Roi. Interesting experiments were made in the realm of industrial prefabrication by Claude Parent and Lionel Schein.

Town planning did not result in the elimination of the fundamentally traditional principle of French architecture. No completely new town has been created, although after the war Auguste Perret was approached for the rebuilding of Le Havre, Jean de Mailly and Serge Mikelian for that of Toulon and Jean Vergnaud for Valenciennes. Marcel M. Lods prepared the master plan for Sotteville-les-Rouen and even Le Corbusier was commissioned to prepare some new plans. There were signs of a beginning of progressive thinking in smaller towns on the west coast but in general the prevailing taste was victorious. A few buildings in Royan show clear influences of Brazilian architecture. The shopping center and the swimming pools by Henri Maillard are in their fundamental conception related to Niemeyer and Burle-Marx.

An important part of French architecture is concentrated in isolated large-scale projects. Besides divers exhibition buildings the Unesco Building by Marcel Breuer, Bernard Zehrfuss and Pier Luigi Nervi must be mentioned as well as the Centre National des Industries et des Techniques in Paris by Camelot, de Mailly and Zehrfuss; the Maison de la Radio in Paris by Henry Bernard; the covered sports arena in Mulhouse by Girardet and Perrin; the Air Terminal Quai by Perlsee; the French-American Hospital at St. Lô by Paul Nelson; the Europa Broadcasting Station by Jean François Guédy; also the market halls in Rheims by Émile Maigrot and in Royan by Simon and Morisseau. All these buildings by leading architects were individual successes in the face of opposition by the official architectural bureaucracy. Important school buildings are those by Beaudouin and Lods in Suresnes; by André Lurçat in Villejuif and more recently those by Heaume and Persitz, Montagné, Robert and Vauzelle.

Commercial and industrial buildings are developing only slowly. Those which are pioneering in their field are the Nuclear Research Works at Marcoule by Badani and Roux-Dorlut, office buildings by Edouard Albert in Paris; the buildings by S. and L. Hartmann at Port Gentil and by Gaston Leclaire in Seremange-Thionville as well as the office buildings by the young Olivier Vaudou at Ivry.

Modern church building received an astonishing impetus during the years between the two extremes of Notre Dame du Rainey (1923) by Auguste Perret and the chapel near Ronchamp (1955) by Le Corbusier. Important designs in this field are by Pinsard, Pingusson, Marchand, Lopez, Lods, Gillet, Hebrard and Galantay. Michel Andrault, who was born in 1926, has won recognition even abroad through his far-sighted and advanced designs.

A decisive contribution to future architecture has been made by Bernard Lafaille, who died in 1957. Since his Pavilion in Zagreb (1936) he has been engaged in problems connected with the suspension roof structure and other dynamic solutions. His efforts have influenced international development considerably; his contribution is not only evident in his designs for exhibition buildings and churches, but also in his participation in projects by other architects, who are indebted to him for the dynamic influence in major buildings. The works by Alain Bourbonnais and Michel Fourtané, who were born in 1925 and 1926, are unthinkable without the achievements by Bernard Lafailles; the same applies to the Tourist Center by Marion Tournon-Bramly and Bernard de la Tour d'Auvergne. It is possible that from these a renewal of French architecture will develop.

SPAIN

An early forerunner of modern architecture in Spain was Arturo Soria y Mata, who with his ribbon town already at the end of the 19th century developed ideas for a new order in the town planning realm. These plans like those of Ebenezer Howard in England and Tony Garnier in France dealt with problems which our present age creates. Through Antonio Gaudi, who for a long time had been misunderstood as a strange inventor of fantastic forms of architecture, Spain made a regional and fascinating contribution to the Jugendstil and to the revival of architecture through the abandonment of wrongly interpreted tradition. Almost the entire work of this far-sighted forerunner of modern architecture is concentrated in Barcelona. Already in 1874 his first house was built in the Calle de las Carolinas. In 1885–89 followed the Guell House and a house in Tangier. Here for the first time his architectural principles can be distinguished: the organic structure of the building and a design form of the architectural elements adapted to their various functions. Between 1900 and 1910 his famous buildings for the Guell Park and the Colonia Guell Church as well as the Mila and Batllo houses were built. His most audacious work which was his main occupation up to his death is, however, the Sagrada Familia, a church of an ecstatic power of expression. Gaudi cannot be reckoned as part of the continual process of the development of modern architecture, but he has made a contribution to it. His certainty in the application of many unusable materials and especially his sense of the functional expression of the building elements which were of a plastic order, have only now produced their full influence.

One of the most important schemes of the new Spanish architecture is the University City of Madrid, which was built about 1930. It consists of three parts, the medical institutes and hospitals, the buildings for the

H. Maillard: School at Royan

FRANCE

scientific and classical faculties with the office of the rectorate, and the blocks for art, architecture and music. The individual blocks are by Modesto Lopez Otero, Pascual Bravo, Agostino Aguirre and Michele de los Santos.

The dominant personality of modern Spanish architecture is Eduardo Torroja. His endeavors were mostly directed towards the full exploitation of the structural possibilities of concrete which have resulted in a new refinement of this material.

The same line of thought was pursued by Candela, who emigrated to Mexico in 1939. Torroja's Sports Arena in Madrid, which he designed in collaboration with Secundino Zuazo Ugalde in 1935, as well as his more recent works like the mighty grandstands of the racecourse at Zarzuela and the Institute for Concrete and Construction at Costillares near Madrid, are outstanding examples of the development of modern form, as are also his churches, bridges and waterworks.

For the young generation Barcelona is the important center besides Madrid. It has become a place where the endeavors of the avant-garde have crystallized. Barcelona is the only place in Spain which can look back on a certain cultural tradition from Gaudi via Picasso and Miro down to Antonio Tapies. With architecture, as is the case with painting, there are a number of young artists who can point to remarkable achievements and some of them are known through international appreciation. Joaquin Selles Codina had built excellent one-family houses already in the thirties. José Luis Sert, who later emigrated to the United States, built a medical laboratory in Barcelona. The young architects Cesar Ortiz de Echague, Raphael de la Joya Castro and Manuel Barbero Rebolledo have built the canteen and games rooms for a factory in Barcelona. The team is working on the plans for a satellite town to Madrid for 30,000 people. They were awarded 1st prize in the international competition of 1957 under the auspices of the Reynolds Foundation for the best architectural use of aluminum.

Oriol Bohigas and José Maria Martorell, both born in 1925, have paid foremost attention to the one-family house and have tried to combine the different architectural forms of Spanish tradition based on climatic conditions with the achievements of the international avant garde. The same can be said of the young architects José M. Garcia de Paredes and Javier Carvajal Ferrer who were able to erect domestic and agricultural buildings and municipal offices. Both were able to represent the new Spanish architecture abroad through their Spanish Pavilion at the 11th Triennale in Milan and through the Spanish War Memorial in Rome. In 1952 an exhibition was held under the name "Group R", which was a collective enterprise by a number of architects which brought together some of the avant-garde's endeavors. Those who were represented in this exhibition were José A. Coderch de Sentmenat and Manuel Valls Vergés, who built houses and factories in Barcelona; Joaquin Gili Moros, who together with Basso designed a publishing house in Barcelona; Antonio de Morages Gallisá, José Pratmarso and José M. Sostres Maluquer.

The social contrasts among the Spanish people are great. The heavy burdens resulting from the Civil War have not yet been overcome completely. Since 1953 Spain has, in return for the establishment of American sea and air bases, been receiving economic help from the U.S.A., a matter which has not remained without influence on the general situation.

AFRICA

In those countries of Africa, which have been for a long time under colonial rule the after-effects of European influence are considerable. The conception of colonial architecture has, however, changed its meaning. European architects are still working in the independent African states, but they appear no longer as delegates of a superior foreign culture. They try to take into account the climate and social conditions and endeavor to express the spirit of the country in its architecture.

For the young states of Africa progress is almost identical with industrial advancement. As regards new building methods, they are still at present dependent on experiences gathered in Europe. It is significant that schools and universities are first on the list among the projects given to foreign architects, but it will not be long before a generation of young Africans has gained the necessary skills for their own further development. Already at the present time there are the beginnings of centers of the new architecture in Africa, which one day may become important for the growth of the continent: Casablanca and Rabat, Algiers and Dakar, Conacry and Abidjan, as well as the university towns of Accra and Ibadan. African architecture has the advantage of being shaped by a social reality. For this formation the architects were able to draw on the social sciences, climatology and the highly specialized methods of construction of Europe. The building of universities and hospitals, housing projects and schools is for the time being the center of attention. Architects from France and Great Britain have done pioneering work in these fields.

In North Africa an architecture of special maturity and fascinating audacity has developed, with roots in France. E. Delaporte designed the hospital, the school and one-family houses at Rabat as well as blocks of apartments in Agadir. Jean Chemineau built representative social institutions for the local administration at Rabat. The old people's home by Souissi, of a simple long horizontal order, as well as apartment buildings by Jean Chemineau, A. Planque and R. Deneux fit well into the face of Rabat.

Casablanca is without doubt a center of African architecture. Most of the important North African architects have their residence in that town. G. Candilis and S. Woods have built apartment houses, Émile Jean Duhon the Hotel Marhaba, Hans Ewerth and Georges Godefroy luxurious villas.

As further important individual buildings must be mentioned the schools by J. F. Zevaco, which together with the earlier circular schools by Camelot had a great influence on the architecture of the country. School and hospital buildings at Boulhout and the Tourists' Aerodrome at Casablanca show the creative gift of the architect Zevaco, who was born in 1916. One of the most important major buildings is the Market Hall in Sidi-bel-Abbès by J. M. Mauri. North Africa's most significant achievement in town planning is the new town of Bournazel, a satellite to Casablanca. Albert Lucas together with a number of younger architects has created a garden city with an impressive solution of the traffic problem.

A further architectural center in North Africa is Algiers, especially through the works of Emery and Miquel. These became known through houses, schools and a factory in Bezons as well as through town planning schemes, of which that for Berrouaghia in Algeria was internationally appreciated. André Studer designed in 1955 a block of apartments of pyramidal shape for Morocco, which constitutes a decisive step in the direction of integrated planning. A competition set by the Moroccan authorities was held in 1956 for the design of low cost apartments. The winner was Gaston Jaubert, who had previously built excellent houses in Casablanca and in Sonk Djemma des Fedelat, the latter in collaboration with Zapasof.

The new architecture of West Africa is concentrated at Conacry and Abidjan. Marcel M. Lods in the Market Hall of Conacry created a dominating focal point for the town. The projected hospital block, which he designed in collaboration with Le Caisne, Aynes and Thierrart, will capably co-ordinate the manifold functions of a large hospital. Guy Lagneau is the architect of an industrial block at Edea in the Cameroons. In Conacry he designed the imposing Hôtel de France in conjunction with Michel Weill and Jean Dimitrijevic, as well as a fully air-conditioned office block with apartments at Conacry, the façade treatment of which is fascinating by the shape of the brise-soleil. Near Conacry R. de Cidrac has built an exemplary housing development for employees of an industrial firm.

Daniel Badani and Pierre Roux-Dorlut designed the administrative building of the French government house at Dakar which is an impressive structure of horizontal proportions with an extravagant entrance hall. The whole creates the impression of a certain heaviness and stressed monumentality. The Hôtel N'Gor in the same town is by Chesneau, Verola and Lenoble. The new appearance of Abidjan is essentially due to the buildings by Henri Chomette, such as the town hall, the market hall in horseshoe shape and a number of office blocks.

Important centers of the new architecture in Africa are Ghana and Nigeria. Ghana's prominent buildings are by James Cubitt, Scott & Partners. The most significant work of this London firm of architects is the Kumasi College of Technology, the country's first school of this kind which was built from 1952 to 1954. The scattered lay-out of the college incorporates lecture halls, laboratories, living quarters, power plant, meeting hall and church. In Sekondi a teachers' seminary, library and school were built, in Accra the Technical Institute, and in Berekum and Jasikan further teachers' seminaries and other educational and administrative buildings. Outstanding examples of the international development are the buildings by James Cubitt, Scott & Partners together with the University Library at Accra by Nickson and Borys, the museum there by Drake & Lasdun with its magnificent aluminum dome, prefabricated in England, and the project for the United States Consulate by Harry Weese.

E. Maxwell Fry and Jane Drew had a fundamental influence on the new architecture in Nigeria. Here, too, a university, that of Ibadan, is a first-rate building. The English architects achieved an architectural form suitable to the local climate, in the various university buildings, the students' dormitory and the library, a long block with typical "breathing" walls, which are a traditional form of construction of the Yoruba people. The London firm of architects, W. H. Watkins, Gray & Partners in collaboration with Ove Arup, the structural engineer, built the hospital in Ibadan, which is also a training hospital for nurses. The whole design and lay-out of Ibadan University can be regarded as one of the most magnificent achievements of the new architecture in Africa and is a convincing proof of the responsible work of European architects in the former colonies.

Further works by Europeans in Africa are the Lome Hospital in Togoland by Crouzat, the National Museum in Salisbury (Rhodesia) by Montgomery and Oldfields, the various office blocks in Leopoldville (Belgian Congo) by Claude Laurens and the works by Ernst May in Nairobi, Moshi and Kisumi. The first noteworthy buildings by African architects are those by George Pace in Ibadan and Kersey D. Moddie in Uganda.

All these buildings prove that Africa is on the way to a new cultural level. Through its own architectural education and its rapidly growing industries Africa's civilization will quickly develop. The close link between architecture and social conditions can be regarded as a happy omen, creating possibilities for fundamentally new conceptions of town planning schemes.

INDIA

In India the erection of a new capital of the Eastern Punjab has become the germinal cell of modern architecture. All powers were concentrated on this goal and famous architects and town planners were called in. Originally the Americans Mayer and Whittlesey together with Matthew Nowicki had been commissioned with the overall planning scheme. After Nowicki's death the Europeans Le Corbusier, Pierre Jeanneret, E. Maxwell Fry and Jane Drew were charged with this task.

Chandigarh lies directly at the spurs of the Himalayas in the middle of a wide plateau. The general conditions of work were extremely unfavorable. There were no modern machines or trained professional workers. The greater part of the work had to be done by unskilled Indian labor. Besides, one had to take into consideration the specific character of the Indian climate, which in that area consists of ten months of hot sunshine and two months of rain. As in other tropical countries the house has to give protection from the sun and keep the rain out, but at the same time, it has to be airy so that the room temperature is tolerable.

The town lies between two rivers which, however, only carry water during the rainy season. Between them is a rectangular network of streets with the administrative center, the Capitol, rising up at the northeastern side. In the center of the grid of streets is the shopping center which is interwoven with green areas, the town hall, the library, the museum and the theatre. The industrial quarter was located at the south east end of the town. Le Corbusier compared the plan of the town with the picture of a man, regarding the administrative center as the head, green spaces and town center as lungs and heart, and the residential areas and the factories as trunk and legs.

A notable characteristic feature of the design for this new town is its noble scale and spaciousness which was achieved in spite of having maximum economy as a basis. The total costs were 35 million dollars. The simplest type of the houses, which were graded according to income groups, costs 620 dollars! The town is, however, by no means a collection of dwellings, shops, factories, offices and civic buildings, but all these various kinds of buildings were grouped together into 25 neighborhoods, each consisting of 128 houses with its own bazaar, hospital, police station, kindergarten, cinema etc. The sound principle, that a conglomeration of virtually perfect living units by no means suffices to form a community, has been recognized and borne in mind. Main works showing Le Corbusier's plastic approach to design are the Law Courts and the Secretariat which houses the entire administration of the town. A particularly important function, in this process of humanizing a town, is the regulation of traffic. The principle of differentiating the road users resulted in Le Corbusier dividing the street system into seven categories:

1 Through roads for fast traffic;
2 Low-lying main roads for town traffic;
3 Speedways for cars only, not accessible to cyclists or pedestrians;
4 Shopping streets without motor traffic;
5 Access roads to the individual neighborhoods for slow traffic;
6 Private ways to the individual houses;
7 Cycle paths and pavements.

Through this way of separating the individual traffic functions each user of a particular road has an equal right and the result is a full utilization of the means of transport.

The entire design is fascinating through the plastic effect of the buildings. The problem of water supply and of the upkeep of the green areas was solved by an artificial dyke and through judicious planting. Le Corbusier said about his town-planning achievement: "The materials for town-planning are the sky, the space, trees, steel and cement in that same order and sequence."

The chief material in Chandigarh is hand-made brick. Steel and reinforced concrete have only been used for the largest buildings, as steel is too rare and therefore too expensive. The outer walls of the majority of the buildings have been left in their raw state. About the time of the building of Chandigarh the term New Brutalism was coined in Europe for a new trend in modern architecture. Without doubt the later works of Le Corbusier can to a considerable extent be linked to that trend whose name only insufficiently describes the phenomenon.

Other works of importance arose in Ahmedabad, where Le Corbusier erected the magnificent museum as well as one-family houses and a co-operative society's building. The American architects Antonin Raymond and Robert E. Alexander have individual buildings in Pondicherry and Madras to their credit.

The building of Chandigarh is one of the perfect examples of the realization of Le Corbusier's theories. Here to a large extent his discovery of the harmony and proportion of building elements has been put into practice. All buildings are based on the modulor, which is a ratio of proportions with unimagined possibilities of design application for the future. In that respect this town planning achievement is of an importance far beyond the boundaries of India. Here, for the first time, one of the most fascinating ideas of the great artist has become reality, and that at a time when Le Corbusier is at the peak of his creative work. The modulor, the universal unit of artistic measurement, has proved to be capable of becoming the key to a new kind of design. This result is an immense step forward into the future of architecture, which may be instrumental in influencing the creativeness of the people for whom it has been designed.

JAPAN

For the Japanese architect, who had lost at the beginning of this century his link with the great tradition of Japanese building, the foremost task was the taking over, at times even the copying, of European and American styles. Japan at that time lay outside architectural decisions. The stage for new development was the U.S.A. and Europe. The foundation for the new Japanese architecture was laid when a group of architects joined forces under the name of "Bunriha Kenchiku-Kai". The leading men of this movement were Ishimoto, Horiguchi and Takizawa. Momentum was added to this force by turning to the great pioneers in Europe: Bunzo Yamaguchi studied under Walter Gropius, Kunio Mayekawa and Junzo Sakakura under Le Corbusier. Later on Mayekawa worked with Antonin Raymond, who along with Gropius, Bruno Taut and Le Corbusier contributed to the formation of the new Japanese architecture. Of vital influence was also Frank Lloyd Wright's Imperial Hotel in Tokyo, which was built of local materials and took specially into account the geological conditions of Japan. The result of all this is the manifold intertwining of European/American architecture with the newly developing one of Japan in recent times. Kiyoshi Ikebe spoke of four stages in which the relationship of Japan to Western architecture developed: 1. imitation, 2. eclecticism, 3. parallel experiments with forms, and 4. reassessment and revival of Japanese architecture from tradition. Ikebe thereby gives us in the shortest formula a summary of Japanese architectural development since the industrial revolution, which started in 1868, down to the very latest results of contemporary architecture.

Sutemi Horiguchi, who was born in 1895, is one of the pioneers. His earliest buildings like the machine hall of the Peace Exhibition in Tokyo date from the nineteen twenties. His building for the Meteorological Station on the Oshima islands (1928) achieved fame; it already shows the clear cubistic forms of European rectangular architecture. The Kikkawa House in Tokyo of two years later is one of the earliest examples of a Japanese dwelling based on reinforced concrete frame construction.

Tetsuro Yoshida (1894–1956) has, through his publications, acquainted the Western world as has no other Japanese architect, with the artistic achievements of his country's architecture of the past. That is why during his later years his work as an architect has been no longer prominent. However, his early buildings, and especially the post offices in Tokyo and Osaka, signify important stages of the new Japanese architecture. The Head Post Office in Tokyo (1931) is a steel frame building with a glazed brick exterior and square window openings, the whole being designed on a generous scale. The Head Post Office in Osaka (1939) shows a wall treatment with greater expanses of glass, the windows being sandwiched between plain surfaces of light-blue bricks. Both buildings are highlights of Japanese architecture which at that time was still in the searching stage.

Mamoru Yamada, the third of the great Japanese architects of the older generation, was born in 1894, the same year as Yoshida. He made his name mainly as an architect of hospitals. The Teishin Hospital in Tokyo, which was built a few years later than Alvar Aalto's wonderful sanatorium at Paimio, and is comparable with the latter work by reason of its functional design, is a masterpiece of Japanese architecture. An even better work is the Welfare Pension Hospital in Tokyo with its Y-shaped plan giving all wings the best possible angle of light. Where the three wings meet the very individualistic glass tower tops the whole like a crown and is accessible through a spiral ramp, enabling the patients to see the panorama of the town. The university hospital of Osaka, completed in 1956, already has extensive parts of the wall surface totally dissolved in glass, with the remaining parts of the façade made up of balconies suitable for the needs of the patients.

The highlights of present day Japanese architecture are the works of Junzo Sakkakura, born in 1904, who with his masterpieces not only tries to combine the spatial strength of Le Corbusier with the formal beauty of Mies van der Rohe, but adds the specific elements of Japanese tradition to this synthesis. Thereby he arrives at a new structural mode of design. The most important work of his earlier years, the Japanese Pavilion for the World Exhibition in Paris of 1937, acquainted Europe with Japan's architecture. The bold design of this early house is even surpassed by the masterpiece of his mature age, the Museum for Modern Art in Kamakura. In this museum, erected in 1951, the synthesis of Japanese tradition and the new discoveries of 20th century architecture has been fully achieved. Some larger projects for a department store, a railway station, a theatre in Tokyo and some residential areas, show the aim of Sakakura to reach beyond the individual building towards a new form of town planning which is today more necessary than ever before.

Kunio Mayekawa built the central office of the Nippon Sogo Bank in Tokyo in 1952 as well as the Kanagawa Library and the Concert Hall in Yokohama, two building projects joined by a connecting passage, which have gained a delicate texture through contrasting areas of glass with pierced brick walls. Here too the building is integrated with a park as in most major works of Japanese architecture. A further building by Kunio Mayekawa is the Fukushima Kyoiku-Kaihan Auditorium, which has a forceful appearance through the projecting wall on a slope and the undulating roof.

Hideo Kosaka is the head of the Planning Department in the Japanese Ministry of Postal Affairs. A large part of the imposing postal buildings may be explained by his activity. His post office at Sendai (1951) is one of the last great Japanese wooden structures. The Post Office Savings Bank at Kyoto was completed in 1955. This building, which has the clarity of a reinforced concrete frame-work combined with the beautiful details of the traditional Japanese house, is harmoniously positioned in the preserved classical garden. In the same year the Art Museum at Aichi was finished.

More recent houses are by Junzo Yoshimura, who like Minoru Yamasaki now works in the U.S.A., Osamu Oe, Katno Andow, Shoji & Masako Hayashi, Kenji Hirose, Yoshio Kasai, Tsotomu Ikuta, Kikutake, Kitadai and Nakayama. Tetsuro Okada built hotels, Ebihara, Taneo Oki and Yutaro Irie factories, Kisaburo Ito, Togo Rakuto and Minoru Ota hospitals. Togo Murano did exemplary work in constructing large department stores. Eminent cultural and educational buildings are by Fuminaja Kiyoto, Murata and Hiroshi Ohe.

Outstanding among the architects of the present day are Takamasa Yoshizaka who, apart from notable one-family houses, built the Japanese Pavilion at the Biennale in Venice (1956), and also Kenzo Tange, who particularly through his buildings in Hiroshima, Numazu and Matsuyama has won recognition even in Europe and America as one of the great structural experts of contemporary architecture. Especially the meeting hall at Matsuyama, a dome-capped circular building with an equally circular annex for exhibitions and administrative purposes, the children's library and the community center in Hiroshima as well as the printing works at Numazu are epoch-making buildings which have led the architects who were at the beginning influenced by Le Corbusier and Gropius to their own independent achievements. The latest works by Kenzo Tange are the municipal administration center in Tokyo and the meeting hall in Shizuoka, which constitute a fascinating variant of the cable roof above a square plan.

OUTLOOK

The architecture of the first half of the 20th century was determined by the polarity of the buildings of Mies van der Rohe and Le Corbusier. Both architects embody the highest form of architectural expression of the time. Both have consistently exploited a certain principle: Mies van der Rohe the structural use of the steel frame and Le Corbusier the tectonic qualities of reinforced concrete. The future development of architecture will be essentially influenced by the work of these two men.

The dynamic trend since the middle of the present century is the commencement of a new phase, which results in placing Mies van der Rohe and Le Corbusier on one plane as distinct from Lafaille, Nowicki, Saarinen and Candela who designed the first buildings expressing this new style. These architects and engineers are united in their endeavor to overcome the limitations of rectangular spatial conceptions in favor of dynamic ones; and they aim at a reduction of the building costs through the use of synthetic materials and rationalized methods of construction. Through the pioneering achievements of engineers and through science and industry the plastic possibilities of present-day architecture have been extended appreciably.

For the architecture of the future new perspectives are evident. The factory-made house will play an important rôle. As one buys a car nowadays, so will one later be buying a house, a completely furnished standardized item made of plastics and glass, poured into moulds and mass manufactured. This, of course, cannot be classified as architecture, but it will materially influence the future development of architecture. Each evolution of technique occurs in accordance with the laws of necessity and can only be mastered if one recognizes its nature and can utilize it. From the possibilities presented by technique noticeable consequences will result in the social realm. The architect cannot and may not be blind to irresistible development. He has to be in a position to control and direct it. The overcoming of difficulties presented by the contemporary situation has at all times been the foremost task of the great master builders.

The spanning of large spaces is no longer a difficulty for the architect. The use of light-weight materials need not be limited to building exhibition halls, but can span entire landscapes and create a new distinctive neighborhood. Appropriate schemes completely capable of realization have already been made on this basis. The architect will thereby be in a position to influence the shaping of our surroundings on a large scale.

We have become aware of the basic conceptions of any buildings, i. e. cave or tent, in a new way through modern technique. These primitive first forms of architecture have been re-discovered in this present age and have become the starting point of a new artistic language of architectural expression. Our age is on the road to a complete volte-face towards the dynamic. This will not only be evident in the numerous forms of temporary abode (hotel, trailer, sleeping car, camp etc.) but the fundamental conception of building itself has become dynamic. This conception no longer recognizes any fixed and unalterable order or discipline, but is looking for transparent enclosures and cells, spatial and social structures, which are related to modern man with his desire for movement, for change.

BIBLIOGRAPHY

Abel, Joseph H. and Severud, Fred. N.: Apartment Houses, New York 1947
Abercrombie, Leslie Patrick: Plan for Greater London, London 1944
Ahlers-Hestermann, Friedrich: Stilwende, Berlin 1941
Argan, Giulio C.: Walter Gropius e la Bauhaus, Roma 1951
– Pier Luigi Nervi, Milano 1955
– Marcel Breuer, Milano 1957
Arup, Ove: Memorandum on Box Frame Construction, London 1944
Ashbee, Charles Robert: Frank Lloyd Wright – Ausgeführte Bauten, Berlin 1911
The Architect Gunnar Asplund, Stockholm 1950
Badovici, Jean: Grandes Constructions, Paris 1931
Baillie Scott, Mackay H.: Houses and Gardens, London 1906
Bauer, Catherine: Modern Housing, Boston and New York 1934
Bazel, K. P. de: Dr. Hendrik Petrus Berlage en zijn werk, Rotterdam 1916
Behrendt, Walter Curt: Der Kampf um den Stil im Kunstgewerbe und in der Architektur, Berlin 1920
– Modern Building, New York 1937
Behrens, Peter: Beziehungen der künstlerischen und technischen Probleme, Berlin 1917
– Das Ethos und die Umlagerung der künstlerischen Probleme, Darmstadt 1920
Bergós, J.: Antonio Gaudi, l'hombre i l'obra, Barcelona 1957
Berlage, Hendrik Petrus: Gedanken über den Stil in der Baukunst, Leipzig 1905
– Grundlagen und Entwicklung der Architektur, Berlin 1908
Bertram, Anthony: The House, a Machine for Living In, London 1935
Bill, Max: Robert Maillart, Zürich 1949
– Form, Basel 1952
– Ludwig Mies van der Rohe, Milano 1955
Blake, Peter: Marcel Breuer, New York 1952
Bloomfield, Paul: William Morris, London 1934
Bloomfield, Reginald: Richard Norman Shaw, London 1940
Boada, J. Puig: El Temple de la Sagrada Familia, Barcelona 1929
Bourgeois, Victor: Architectures 1922–1952, Brussels 1952
Breuer, Marcel: Sun and Shadow, New York 1957
Brinckmann, Albert Erich: Platz und Monument, Berlin 1908
– Baukunst – Die künstlerischen Werte im Werk des Architekten, Tübingen 1956
Calzada, Andre: Historia de la Arquitectura Espanola, Barcelona 1933
Carver, Norman F.: Form and Space in Japanese Architecture, Tokyo 1956
Caudill, William W.: Toward Better School Design, New York 1954
Cheney, Sheldon: The New World Architecture, New York 1930
Christ-Janer, Albert: Eliel Saarinen, Chicago 1949
Cirlot, Juan Eduardo: El Arte de Gaudi, Barcelona 1950
Condit, Carl W.: The Rise of the Skyscraper, Chicago 1952
Conrady, Ch. und Thibaut, R.: Paul Hankar, 1923
Le Corbusier: Vers une Architecture, Paris 1923
– Urbanisme, Paris 1925
– Une Maison – un Palais, Paris 1929
– Precisions sur un état présent de l'architecture et de l'urbanisme, Paris 1930
– Des Canons, des Munitions, Paris 1938
– When the Cathedrals Were White, New York 1947
– Grundfragen des Städtebaus, Stuttgart 1954

Le Corbusier: The Modulor, London 1955
– Ronchamp, Stuttgart 1957
Le Corbusier und Jeanneret, Pierre: Oeuvre Complete, Erlenbach-Zürich seit 1930
Costa, Lucio: Consideracoes sobre arte contemporanea, Rio de Janeiro 1952
Cremers, P. J.: Peter Behrens, Essen 1928
Dahinden, Justus: Versuch einer Standortbestimmung der Gegenwartsarchitektur, Zürich 1956
Damaz, P.: Art in European Architecture, New York 1956
Davies, Richard Llewelyn and Petty, D. J.: Building Elements, London 1957
W. M. Dudok – Life and Work, Amsterdam 1954
Endell, August: Die Schönheit der großen Stadt, Stuttgart 1908
Fisker, Kay und Yerbury, F. R.: Modern Danish Architecture, London 1927
Fitch, James Marston: American Building, Boston 1948
Flügge, W.: Statik und Dynamik der Schalen, Berlin 1941
Gantner, Joseph: Grundformen der europäischen Stadt, Wien 1928
Garnier, Tony: Une Cité Industrielle, Paris 1917
Geddes, Patrick: Cities in Evolution, London 1915
Gibberd, Frederick: The Architecture in England, London 1938
– Town Design, London 1952
Giedion, Siegfried: Bauen in Frankreich, Berlin 1928
– Befreites Wohnen, Zürich und Leipzig 1929
– Time, Space and Architecture, Cambridge (USA) 1941
– Mechanisation Takes Command, New York 1948
– Ein Jahrzehnt moderner Architektur, Zürich 1954
– Walter Gropius, Stuttgart 1954
– Architektur und Gemeinschaft, Hamburg 1956
Ginzburger, Roger: Neues Bauen in der Welt – Frankreich, Wien 1930
Gloag, John und Derck Bridgewater: Cast Iron in Architecture, London 1948
Glück, Franz: Adolf Loos, Paris 1931
Goodwin, Philip L.: Brazil Builds, New York 1943
Gratama, J.: Dr. H. P. Berlage Bouwmeester, Rotterdam 1925
Grimme, Karl Maria: Peter Behrens und seine Wiener akademische Meisterschule, Wien 1930
Grohmann, Will: Bildende Kunst und Architektur, Berlin 1953
Gropius, Walter: Internationale Architektur, München 1925
– Bauhausbauten Dessau, München 1930
– The New Architecture and the Bauhaus, London 1935
– Rebuilding Our Communities, Chicago 1945
– Scope of Total Architecture, New York 1954
Guarneri, L.: L'Evoluzione Dell'Architettura Moderna, Milano 1954
Hajual-Konyi, K.: Concrete, London 1948
Hamlin, Talbot: Architecture Through the Ages, New York 1944
– Forms and Functions of Twentieth-Century Architecture, New York 1952
Handisyde, Cecil C.: Building Materials, London 1950
Harada, Jiro: The Lesson of Japanese Architecture, Boston 1954
Hart, Franz: Skelettbauten, München 1956
Hebebrand, Werner: Contemporary architecture and city planning in West Germany, New York 1957
Hempel, E.: Geschichte der deutschen Baukunst, München 1956
Heuss, Theodor: Hans Poelzig, Berlin 1939
Hilberseimer, Ludwig: The Nature of Cities, Chicago 1955
– Mies van der Rohe, Chicago 1956
Hitchcock, Henry Russell: Modern Architecture – Romanticism and Reintegration, New York 1929

Hitchcock, Henry Russell: J. J. P. Oud, Paris 1931
- The Architecture of H. H. Richardson and his Times, New York 1936
- In the Nature of Materials – The Buildings of Frank Lloyd Wright, New York 1942
- Latin American Architecture since 1945, New York 1955
- Henry Russell and Johnson, Philip: The International Style, New York 1932
Hoeber, Fritz: Peter Behrens, München 1913
Hoffmann, Hubert: Neue deutsche Architektur, Stuttgart 1955
Holme, C. G., Hrsg.: Industrial Architecture, London 1935
Horiguchi, Sutemi: Architectural Beauty in Japan, Tokyo 1955
Horta, Victor: L'Enseignement architectural et l'Architecture Moderne, Brussels 1926
Howarth, Thomas: Charles Rennie Mackintosh and the Modern Movement, London 1952
Hudnut, Joseph: The three Lambs of Modern Architecture, Ann Arbor 1952
Jamot, Paul: Auguste et Gustave Perret et l'architecture du beton armé, Paris 1927
Johnson, Philip: Machine Art, New York 1934
- Mies van der Rohe, New York 1947
Kaufmann, Edgar Jr.: Louis Sullivan and the Architecture of Free Enterprise, Chicago 1956
Kaufmann, Emil: Von Ledoux bis zu Le Corbusier, Wien 1933
- Architecture in the Age of Reason, Cambridge (USA) 1956
Keim, Jean A.: La Tour Eiffel, Paris 1950
Kidder-Smith, G. E.: Switzerland Builds, New York 1950
- Sweden Builds, New York 1957
Kleiner, L.: Josef Hoffmann, Berlin 1927
Koehler und Luckhardt: Lichtarchitektur, Berlin 1956
Koike, Shinji: Contemporary Architecture in Japan, Tokyo 1956
Krakstroem, E.: Nordisk Arkitektur 1950–1954, Helsinki 1955
Kulka, Heinrich: Adolf Loos, Wien 1931
Kuyck, Hugo van: Modern Belgian Architecture, New York 1948
Labo, Mario: Giuseppe Terragni, Milano 1947
Lafaille, Bernard: Anwendung von Schalen im Stahlbau, Berlin 1938
Lanchester, Henry Vaughan: The Art of Town Planning, New York 1925
Lanyi, Richard: Adolf Loos, Wien 1931
Laurent, Marcel: L'Architecture et la Sculpture en Belgique, Brussels and Paris 1928
Lenning, Henry F.: The Art Nouveau, Den Haag 1951
Lethaby, W. R.: Philip Webb and his Work, London 1925
Lindner, Werner: Bauten der Technik, Berlin 1927
El Lissitzky: Die Rekonstruktion der Architektur in der Sowjetunion, Leipzig 1930
Lodders, Rudolf: Industriebau und Architekt und die gegenseitige Beeinflussung, Hamburg 1946
- Von der Persönlichkeit des Architekten, Hamburg 1948
Loos, Adolf: Ins Leere gesprochen, Berlin 1925
- Trotzdem, Innsbruck 1931
Lucas, Albert: La Cité de Bournazel, Casablanca 1956
Lundgren, H.: Cylindrical Shells, Kopenhagen 1951
Lux, Joseph August: Otto Wagner, Berlin 1919
- Josef Maria Olbrich, Berlin 1919
Madsen, Stephan Tschudi: Sources of Art Nouveau, Oslo 1956
Maldonado, Tomas: Max Bill, Buenos Aires 1955
Magnee: W. M. Dudok, Amsterdam 1954
Malkiel-Jirmounsky, M.: Les tendances de l'architecture contemporaine, Paris 1930
Marilaun, Karl: Adolf Loos, Wien 1923

Markalaus, B.: Adolf Loos, Wien 1931
McAndrew, J.: Alvar Aalto, New York 1938
Mebes, Paul: Um 1800, München 1920
Meeks, Caroll L. V.: The Railway Station, London 1957
Mendelsohn, Erich: Das Gesamtschaffen des Architekten, Berlin 1930
- Neues Haus, Neue Welt, Berlin 1932
- Three Lectures on Architecture, Berkeley 1944
Meyer, Alfred G.: Eisenbauten, Esslingen 1907
Meyer, Peter: Moderne Architektur und Tradition, Zürich 1928
Michaels, Leonard: Contemporary Structure in Architecture, New York 1950
Mills, Edward D.: The Modern Factory, London 1951
- The New Architecture in Great Britain, London 1953
- The Modern Church, London 1956
Mindlin, Henrique E.: Neues Bauen in Brasilien, München 1957
Minuccio, Gaetano: Scuole, Milano, 1936
Moholy-Nagy, Laszlo: Vom Material zur Architektur, München 1928
- The New Vision, New York 1930
- Vision in Motion, Chicago 1947
Mondrian, Piet: Neue Gestaltung, München 1924
Morrison, Hugh: Louis Sullivan – Prophet of Modern Architecture, New York 1935
Moser, Werner M.: Frank Lloyd Wright, Winterthur 1952
Mujica, Francisco: History of the Skyscraper, Paris 1929
Mumford, Lewis: Sticks and Stones, New York 1924
- Technics and Civilisation, New York 1934
- The Culture of Cities, New York 1944
Muthesius, Hermann: Architektonische Zeitbetrachtungen, Berlin 1900
- Die englische Baukunst der Gegenwart, Leipzig 1900
- Stilarchitektur und Baukunst, Mülheim-Ruhr 1902
- Das englische Haus, Berlin 1908
Myers, I. E.: Mexico's Modern Architecture, New York 1952
Nelson, Paul: La Maison Suspendue, Paris 1939
Nervi, Pier Luigi: Arte o scienca del costruire, Roma 1945
- Costruire correttamente, Milano 1955
Nestler, Paolo: Neues Bauen in Italien, München 1954
Neuenschwander, E. und C.: Finnish Architecture and Alvar Aalto, New York 1954
Neufert, Ernst: Bauentwurfslehre, Berlin 1936
Neutra, Richard: Neues Bauen in der Welt – Amerika, Wien 1930
- Survival Through Design, New York 1954
- Mensch und Wohnen, Stuttgart 1956
Nickel, Richard S.: The Architecture of Adler and Sullivan, New York 1956
Nicoletti, Manfredi: Raimondo D'Aronco, Milano 1955
Osthaus, Karl Ernst: Van de Velde, Hagen 1920
Otto, Frei: Das hängende Dach, Berlin 1954
Oud, J. J. P.: Ja und Nein, Potsdam 1924
- Holländische Architektur, München 1926
Papadaki, Stamo: Le Corbusier, New York 1948
- The Works of Oscar Niemeyer, New York 1950
- Oscar Niemeyer – Works in Progress, New York 1956
Parkins, M. F.: City Planning in Soviet Russia, Chicago 1953
Peabody, Dean: The Design of Reinforced Concrete Structures, New York 1946
Pedersen, Johan: Arkitekten Arne Jacobsen, Kopenhagen 1956
Pellicer, A. Cirici: La Sagrada Familia, Barcelona 1950
Pevsner, Nikolaus: Pioneers of the Modern Movement, London 1936
- An Outline of European Architecture, London 1945

Pevsner, Nikolaus: Charles Rennie Mackintosh, Milano 1950
– High Victorian Design, London 1951
– Englishness of English Art, London 1956
– Europäische Architektur, München 1957
Pico, Agnoldomenico: Nuova Architettura nel Mondo, Milano1938
Platz, Gustav Adolf: Die Baukunst der neuesten Zeit, Berlin 1927
Ponten, Josef: Architektur die nicht gebaut wurde, Stuttgart 1925
Ponti, Gio: Amate l'architettura, Genova 1957
Prevost, Jean: Eiffel, Paris 1929
Ràfols, Josep F.: Antonio Gaudi, Barcelona 1928
Randolph, W.: A Century of English Architecture, London 1939
Rasch, Heinz und Bodo: Wie Bauen? Stuttgart 1929
Rimpl, H.: Die geistigen Grundlagen der Baukunst unserer Zeit,
    München 1953
Riphahn,Wilhelm: Neue Werkkunst, Berlin 1927
Rogers, Ernesto N.: Raimondo D'Aronco, Milano 1955
– Pier Luigi Nervi, Stuttgart 1956
Roth, Alfred: The New Architecture, Erlenbach-Zürich 1946
– The New School, Zürich 1950
Saarinen, Eliel: The City, New York 1945
– Search for Form, New York 1949
Salvisberg, Otto Rudolf: Nosokomeion, Stuttgart 1934
Sartoris, Alberto: Gli elementi dell'architettura funzionale, Milano
    1935
– Sant'Elia e l'architettura futurista, Roma 1943
– Introduzione alla architettura moderna, Milano 1949
– Encyclopedie de l'architecture Nouvelle, Milano 1954
Scharoun,Hans u.a.:Handbuch moderner Architektur,Berlin 1956
Scheffler, Karl: Moderne Baukunst, Berlin 1907
– Die Architektur der Großstadt, Berlin 1913
Schuhmacher, Adolf: Otto Rudolf Salvisberg, Stuttgart 1935
Schumacher, Fritz: Atomphysik und Architektur, Hamburg 1948
– Srömungen in deutscher Baukunst seit 1800, Köln 1955
Scully, Vincent J.: The Shingle Style, New Haven 1955
Sert, Jose Luis: Can Our Cities Survive? Cambridge (USA) 1942
Severud, Fred und Merrill: The Bomb, Survival and You, New
    York 1955
Sheppard, Richard: Cast Iron in Building, London 1945
Steinmann, David B.: The Builders of the Bridge, New York 1945
Stubblebine, Jo: The Northwest Architecture of Pietro Belluschi,
    New York 1953
Sullivan,Louis:A System of Architectural Ornament,New York1924
– The Autobiography of an Idea, New York 1926
– Kindergarten Chats, New York 1947
Taut, Bruno: Die Auflösung der Städte, Hagen 1920
– Modern Architecture, London 1929
Thiersch, M.: Wir fingen einfach an, München 1954
Torroja, Eduardo: Razon y Ser de los Tipos Estructurales, Madrid
    1957

Tubbs, Ralph: Living in Cities, London 1942
– The Englishman Builds, London 1945
Velde, Henry van de: Die Renaissance im modernen Kunstge-
    werbe, Berlin 1901
– Der neue Stil, Weimar 1906
– Der neue Stil in Frankreich, Berlin und Paris 1925
– Vie et Mort de la Colonne, Brussels 1942
– Zum neuen Stil, München 1955
Veronesi, Giulia: Tony Garnier, Milano 1948
– Josef Maria Olbrich, Milano 1948
Vischer, Julius und Hilberseimer, Ludwig: Beton als Gestalter,
    Stuttgart 1928
Vogt-Goeknil, Ulya: Architektonische Grundbegriffe und Um-
    raumerlebnis, Zürich 1951
Volkart, H.: Schweizer Architektur, Ravensburg 1951
Wagner, Martin: Das wachsende Haus, Stuttgart 1932
Wagner, Otto: Moderne Architektur, Wien 1895
– Die Großstadt, Wien 1911
– Die Qualität des Baukünstlers, Leipzig und Wien 1912
Weiser, Armand: Josef Hoffmann, Genf 1930
Westerdahl, E.: Mathias Göritz, Barcelona 1949
Whittick, Arnold: Eric Mendelsohn, London 1940
– European Architecture in the 20th Century, Lon-
    don 1950
Wijdeveld, Henricus Theodorus, Hrsg.: The Life-work of the
    American Architect Frank Lloyd Wright, Sandpoort 1925
Winkler, Robert: Architect's Houses, New York 1956
Wright, Frank Lloyd: Ausgeführte Bauten und Entwürfe, Berlin
    1910
– Modern Architecture, Princeton 1931
– The Disappearing City, New York 1932
– An Autobiography, New York 1943
– When Democracy Builds, Chicago 1945
– The Natural House, New York 1954
– A Testament, New York 1957
Wright, Henry: Rehousing Urban America, New York 1935
Yorke, Francis Reginald Stevens: The Modern House, London
    1935
Yorke, F. R. S. and Gibberd, F.: The Modern Flat, London 1937
Yoshida, Tetsuro: Japanische Architektur, Tübingen 1952
– Das japanische Wohnhaus, Tübingen 1954
– Der japanische Garten, Tübingen 1957
Zevi, Bruno: Verso un'architettura organica, Torino 1945
– Vita e opere di Louis H. Sullivan, Poligno 1947
– Saper vedere l'architettura, Torino 1948
– Erik Gunnar Asplund, Milano 1949
– Storia dell'architettura moderna, Torino 1953
– Frank Lloyd Wright, Milano 1954
– Architecture as Space, New York 1957

Correction: Page 192 shows a team-work of the architects Rafael G. de Castro Peña and Javier Carvajal Ferrer.

SOURCES OF PHOTOGRAPHS

Aero-photo Nederland, Rotterdam, 139 / C. Ala 87, 88, 89 / L. L. Aragon 86 / Artis, Dakar, 208 / Photo Associates 60 / Barsotti, Florence, 180, 181 / J. Biaugeaud, Arcueil, 182, 189, 191 / Brennero, Rom, 172, 173 / G. Burg, Rotterdam, 144, 145 / De Burgh Galwey 134, 135 / J. Calvo, Madrid, 192 / Casali, Milan, 177 / Clari, Milan, 175 / L. Chmel, Vienna, 169 / V. Cornelius, Amsterdam, 140 / H. Dittmann, Stockholm, 120 / Doeser, Laren, 136 / C. Eames, Venice, 69 / R. Eimke, Düsseldorf, 60, 65 / R. Erskine, Drottingholm, 122, 123 / Fotogramma, Milan, 178, 179 / V. Frama 106 / L. Freedman, New York, 68 / P. Gasparini 98, 99 / M. Gautherat 108 / E. Hartmann, Vienna, 171 / Hedrich-Blessing, Chicago, 62, 63 / Heidersberger, Brunswick, 155 / M. Hellstern, Zürich, 162, 163, 168 / Henrot 187 / Hess, Rio de Janeiro, 102, 103 / Hirayama 226, 233 / P. Hübotter, Hanover, 156 / Hubmann 170 / G. Ifert 185 / K. E. Jacobs, Berlin, 111 / Jaenecke und Samuelson, Malmö, 121 / H. Kaschinski, Münster, 151 / Khopker's Studio, Ahmedabad, 221 / Kidder Smith, New York, 112, 113 / Korab 184 / M. Lacroix, Casablanca, 210, 211 / J. Maltby, London, 126 / Martinotti 174 / Mas, Barcelona, 12 / U. Meisel, Dallas, 61 / A. Michel 109 / W. Milwaukee, Detroit, 74, 75 / S. Molina 78, 79, 80, 81 / F. Murasawa 227 / E. M. van Ojen, The Hague, 137 / J. R. Pantlin, Radlett, 131 / Gebr. Paysan, Stuttgart, 154 / M. Petersen 119 / A. Pfau, Mannheim, 150, 153 / P. Pitt, Southampton, 128, 130 / G. Prats, Barcelona, 194 / Publicam, Hilversum, 142 / F. Rausser, Berne, 167 / Roos, Helsinki, 114, 115 / Sergysels und Dietens, Brussels, 146, 147 / Servicio de Fotografia y Cinematografia, Venezuela, 90, 91, 92, 94, 95 / J. Shulman, Los Angeles, 65 / F. Stoedtner, Düsseldorf, 11, 12, 13, 14 / E. Stoller 70, 71, 72, 73 / Strüwing, Falae, 118 / Wm. Toomey 133 / E. Torihata 234, 235 / E. Troeger, Hamburg, 158 / R. d'Ursle, Brussels, 148 / S. Vandercom 149 / J. Versnel, Amsterdam, 138, 141, 143 / Wainwright 127 / Wehn 110 / C. Westwood, Weybridge, 129

PLATES

Frank Lloyd Wright: Office Block at Bartlesville

USA

Frank Lloyd Wright: Factory at Racine, Wisconsin

USA

USA

Frank Lloyd Wright: House near Madison, Wisconsin

59

Harrison & Abramovitz: Alcoa Building, Pittsburgh

USA

Harrison & Abramovitz: Bank Building at Dallas, Texas

USA

Mies van der Rohe: Point Blocks, Chicago

USA

Mies van der Rohe: Crown Hall, Illinois Institute of Technology, Chicago

USA

USA

Marcel Breuer: "Robinson House" near Williamstown, Massachusetts

Richard Neutra: "Kronish House" at Beverly Hills, California

USA

Skidmore, Owings & Merill (Gordon Bunshaft): "Lever House", New York

USA

USA

Skidmore, Owings & Merrill (Gordon Bunshaft): Bank Building at New York

Paul Rudolph: Holiday House in Florida

USA

Philip Johnson: "Wiley House" at New Canaan, Connecticut

USA

J. M. Pei: Mile High Centre in Denver, Colorado

USA

J. M. Pei: Mile High Centre in Denver, Colorado

USA

USA

Eero Saarinen: General Motors Technical Centre, near Detroit

Eero Saarinen: General Motors Technical Centre, near Detroit

USA

Nowicki, Deitrick and Severud: Exhibition Hall at Raleigh, North Carolina

USA

Nowicki, Deitrick and Severud: Exhibition Hall at Raleigh, North Carolina

Lazo, Pani, de la Mora & Partners: University Town, Mexico City,
Natural Science Faculty and "Auditorium Maximum"

MEXICO

MEXICO

Lazo, Pani, de la Mora & Partners: University Town, Mexico City, Faculty for Philosophy

Lazo, Pani, de la Mora & Partners: University Town, Mexico City, Faculty for Engineering

MEXICO

MEXICO

Lazo, Pani, de la Mora & Partners: University Town, Mexico City, Faculty of Law

M. Cetto: House in Mexico City

MEXICO

MEXICO

A. H. Alvarez: House in Mexico City

E. C. Tamborrel: House in Mexico City

MEXICO

MEXICO

E. C. Tamborrel: House in Mexico City

MEXICO

De la Mora & Candela: Chapel at San José del Altillo, Coyoacan

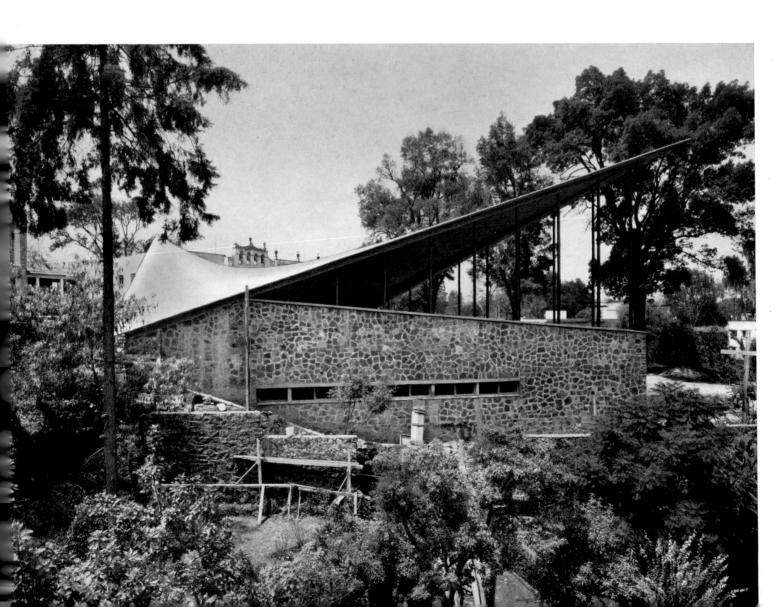

F. Candela: Interior of Church, Mexico City

MEXICO

Reyna & Candela: Laboratory for Radiographic Research, University of Mexico City

MEXICO

C. R. Villanueva: Central Library of the University Town, Caracas

VENEZUELA

VENEZUELA

C. R. Villanueva: Assembly Hall of the University Town, Caracas

C. R. Villanueva: Administrative Block, University Town, Caracas

VENEZUELA

C. R. Villanueva: Ramp in the Assembly Hall, University Town, Caracas

VENEZUELA

C. R. Villanueva: Ramp leading to the Balcony of the Assembly Hall, University Town, Caracas

H. Arp & M. Manaure: Wall treatment in the University Town, Caracas (sculpture by Arp)

VENEZUELA

P. Navarro: Mural in the University Town, Caracas

VENEZUELA

C. R. Villanueva: The Faculty of Architecture & Town Planning, University Town, Caracas

VENEZUELA

C. R. Villanueva: The Faculty of Architecture & Town Planning, University Town, Caracas

VENEZUELA

BRAZIL

R. Levi: Country Villa at São José dos Campos

R. Levi: Cancer Hospital in São Paulo

BRAZIL

BRAZIL

F. Bolonha: Housing Estate on Paqueta

F. Bolonha: Housing Estate on Paqueta

L. Korngold: Office Block in São Paulo

BRAZIL

F. A. Regis: Administrative Building at Salvador, Bahia

BRAZIL

O. Redig de Campos: Weekend House at Petropolis

BRAZIL

BRAZIL

O. Redig de Campos: Weekend House at Petropolis

A. E. Reidy: Housing Estate in Gavea

BRAZIL

O. Redig de Campos: Indoor Swimming Bath with Bar at Petropolis

Alvar Aalto: Sanatorium at Paimio, near Turku, Finland

SCANDINAVIA

E. G. Asplund: Crematorium near Stockholm

SCANDINAVIA

A. Ervi: "Porthania" University, Helsinki

SCANDINAVIA

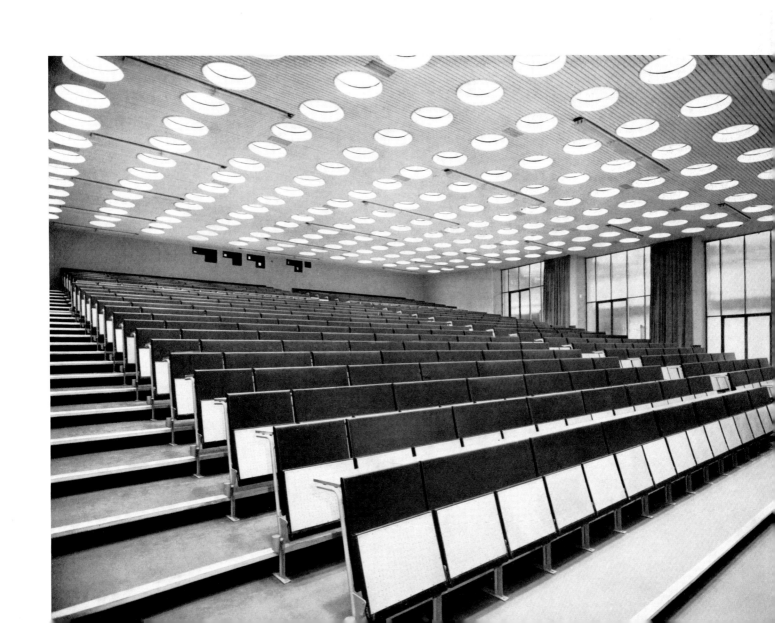

K. & H. Siren: House at Otalaakso, Finland

SCANDINAVIA

SCANDINAVIA

C. Norberg-Schulz: The architect's own house at Vettakollen, Norway

E. & N. Koppel: School at Gladsaxe, Denmark

SCANDINAVIA

SCANDINAVIA

M. Ahlgren: Underground Station at Vällingby, Stockholm

Jaenecke & Samuelson: Housing Estate at Malmö, Sweden

SCANDINAVIA

SCANDINAVIA

R. Erskine: House at Skövde, Västergötland, Sweden

R. Erskine: Factory at Fors, Dalarna, Sweden

SCANDINAVIA

GREAT BRITAIN

Ralph Tubbs: "Dome of Discovery", Festival of Britain, London 1951

Matthew & Martin, L. C. C. Architect's Department; Peter Moro, Associate: Concert Hall,
Festival of Britain, London 1951

GREAT BRITAIN

Skinner, Bailey and Lubetkin: Blocks of Flats in London

GREAT BRITAIN

GREAT BRITAIN

Frederick Gibberd: "The Lawn" Housing Estate, Harlow New Town, Essex

Yorke, Rosenberg & Mardall: School at Stevenage, Hertfordshire (Sculpture by Henry Moore)

GREAT BRITAIN

GREAT BRITAIN

Yorke, Rosenberg & Mardall: School in Essex

Powell & Moya: "Mayfield" School at Putney, London

GREAT BRITAIN

Powell & Moya: "Churchill Gardens" Blocks of Flats at Pimlico, London

GREAT BRITAIN

Drake & Lasdun: School at Paddington, London

GREAT BRITAIN

GREAT BRITAIN

R. H. Matthew: Air Terminal at Turnhouse, Edinburgh

A. & P. Smithson: School at Hunstanton, Norfolk

GREAT BRITAIN

GREAT BRITAIN

A. & P. Smithson: School at Hunstanton, Norfolk

G. Rietveld: House at Utrecht

NETHERLANDS

Van Tijen & Maaskant: Block of Flats at Rotterdam

NETHERLANDS

Breuer, Elzas and Schwartzman, van den Broek and Bakema: Centre of Rotterdam with Departmental
Store "De Bijenkorf" and the Lijnbaan Quarter

NETHERLANDS

G. Rietveld: Pavilion for Sculpture, Arnhem

NETHERLANDS

NETHERLANDS

Maaskant and Krijgsman: Blocks of Flats at Rotterdam

Van den Broek & Bakema: Departmental Store, Rotterdam

NETHERLANDS

NETHERLANDS

Breuer, Elzas & Schwartzman: "De Bijenkorf" Departmental Store, Rotterdam

H. Haan: Country Villa at Hillegersberg

NETHERLANDS

A. and J. Polak: Factory at Gembloux, near Namur

BELGIUM

H. van Kuyck: Office Block at Brussels

BELGIUM

Montois & Courtois: House at Ixelles, Brussels

BELGIUM

C. L. Brodzki: House at Linkebeek

BELGIUM

Gerhard Weber: National Theatre, Mannheim

GERMANY

GERMANY

P. Schneider-Esleben: Multi-storey Garage at Düsseldorf

L. Götz: Petrol Station at Wiesbaden

GERMANY

GERMANY

Abel & Gutbrod: "Lieder-Halle" at Stuttgart

F. W. Kraemer: Factory at Brunswick

GERMANY

Hübotter & Romero: Terrace House at Kirchrode, Hannover

GERMANY

P. Schneider-Esleben: "Baumberg" Housing Estate near Düsseldorf

GERMANY

B. Hermkes: "Philips" Tower at Hamburg

GERMANY

Otto, Lohs, Bubner & Frank: Tent structure over Dancing Fountain
at the Federal Garden Exhibition, Cologne 1957

GERMANY

M. Schlup: Watch Factory at Lengnau, near Biel

SWITZERLAND AND AUSTRIA

M. Schlup: Watch Factory at Lengnau, near Biel

SWITZERLAND AND AUSTRIA

E. Gisel: School at Zürich

SWITZERLAND AND AUSTRIA

E. Gisel: School at Zürich

SWITZERLAND AND AUSTRIA

J. Dahinden: House at Dietikon, Zürich

SWITZERLAND AND AUSTRIA

J. Dahinden: Summer House on the Rigi, Lake of Lucerne

SWITZERLAND AND AUSTRIA

O. H. Senn: House at St. Prex, Lake of Geneva

SWITZERLAND AND AUSTRIA

E. Gisel: Park Theatre at Grenchen, near Biel

SWITZERLAND AND AUSTRIA

C. Holzmeister: "Kammerspiel-Haus" at Linz, Austria

SWITZERLAND AND AUSTRIA

Rainer & Auböck: Prefabricated Housing Estate, Vienna

SWITZERLAND AND AUSTRIA

R. Rainer: Studio House at Grinzing, Vienna

SWITZERLAND AND AUSTRIA

Pier Luigi Nervi: Hangar near Orbetello, Tuscany

ITALY

ITALY

Pier Luigi Nervi: Hangar near Orvieto, Umbria

I. Gardella: Museum of Modern Art, Milan

ITALY

ITALY

I. Gardella: Museum of Modern Art, Milan

L. Galmozzi: House at Lecco, Northern Italy

ITALY

ITALY

I. & L. Parisi: House at Brusimpiano

ITALY

I. & L. Parisi: Park Library, Milan

I. & L. Parisi: Park Library, Milan

ITALY

Gori, Ricci, Savioli & Brizzi: Flower Market at Pescia, near Lucca

ITALY

ITALY

Gori, Ricci, Savioli & Brizzi: Flower Market at Pescia, near Lucca

Boileau and Labourdette: Energy Station near Nantes

FRANCE

FRANCE

Badani and Roux-Dorlut: Nuclear Power Station at Marcoule

A. Wogenscky: House near Paris

FRANCE

FRANCE

A. Wogenscky: House near Paris

FRANCE

H. Maillard: School at Royan

P. Ohnenwald: School at St. Denis

FRANCE

Vaudou and Jausserand: Office Building at Ivry

FRANCE

H. Maillard: Shopping Centre at Royan

FRANCE

Camelot, de Mailly and Zehrfuss: Centre for Industry and Technique at Paris

FRANCE

F. J. Carvajal Ferrer: Block of Flats, Madrid

SPAIN

Coderch de Sentmenat & Valls Vergés: Block of Flats, Barcelona

SPAIN

J. L. Sert: Hospital at Barcelona

SPAIN

Basso & Gili: Publishing Firm's Building, Barcelona

SPAIN

Martorell & Bohigas: House at Barcelona

SPAIN

J. M. Sostres Maluguer: House at Barcelona

SPAIN

J. M. Sostres Maluguer: House at Barcelona

SPAIN

Torroja, Dominguez & Arniches: Grand Stand at the Racecourse, Zarzuela

SPAIN

Torroja, Dominguez & Arniches: Racecourse at Zarzuela

SPAIN

AFRICA

Ernst May: Aga Khan School at Kisumi, Kenya

Ernst May: Aga Khan School at Kisumi, Kenya (part of the class-room block)

AFRICA

Maxwell Fry & Jane Drew: Students' Hostel, University of Ibadan, Nigeria

AFRICA

Maxwell Fry & Jane Drew: Students' Hostel, University of Ibadan, Nigeria

AFRICA

Maxwell Fry & Jane Drew: Students' Hostel, University of Ibadan, Nigeria

AFRICA

Badani and Roux-Dorlut: Administrative Office at Dakar

AFRICA

AFRICA

G. Lagneau: "Hôtel de France", Conacry, French Guinea

H. Ewerth: House near Casablanca, Morocco

AFRICA

AFRICA

H. Ewerth: House near Casablanca, Morocco

Drake & Lasdun: National Museum at Accra, Ghana

AFRICA

AFRICA

Drake & Lasdun: Bank Building at Takoradi, Ghana

INDIA

Le Corbusier: Law Courts at Chandigarh, Punjab

P. Jeanneret: House of a Cabinet Minister, Chandigarh, Punjab

INDIA

INDIA

P. Jeanneret: House of a Cabinet Minister, Chandigarh, Punjab

Chaudhri: School of Engineering, Chandigarh, Punjab

INDIA

Maxwell Fry & Jane Drew: Houses at Chandigarh, Punjab

INDIA

INDIA

Maxwell Fry & Jane Drew: House at Chandigarh, Punjab

INDIA

Le Corbusier: Headquarters of the Mill Owners Union at Ahmedabad, Bombay Province

Le Corbusier: Headquarters of the Mill Owners Union at Ahmedabad, Bombay Province

INDIA

Le Corbusier: Secretariat at Chandigarh, Punjab

INDIA

H. Kosaka: Postal Savings Bank at Kyoto (View from garden)

JAPAN

JAPAN

M. Yamada: Hospital at Tokyo

JAPAN

K. Mayekawa: Library and Concert Hall at Yokohama

K. Mayekawa: Library and Concert Hall at Yokohama

JAPAN

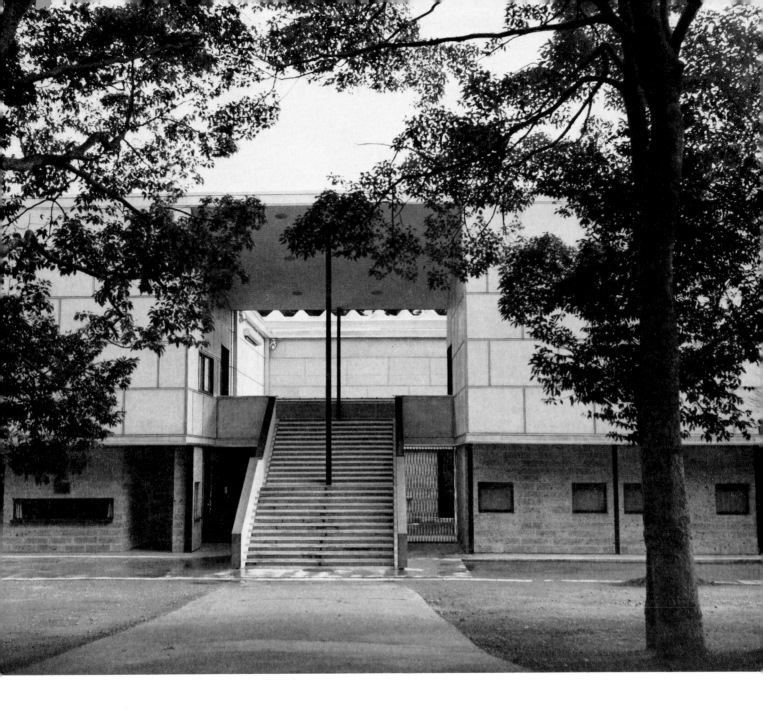

J. Sakakura: Museum of Modern Art at Kamakura

JAPAN

JAPAN

J. Sakakura: Museum of Modern Art at Kamakura

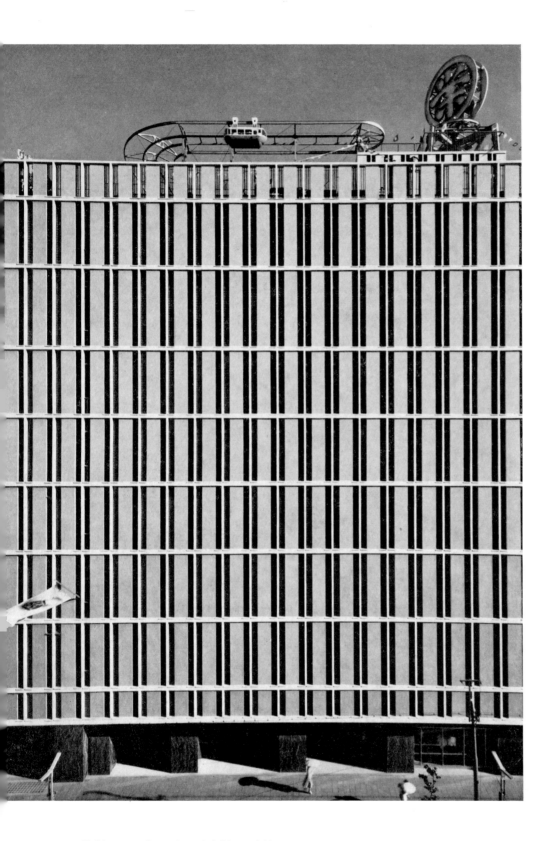

T. Murano: Departmental Store at Nagoya

JAPAN

T. Murano: Departmental Store at Nagoya

JAPAN

K. Tange: Hall of Peace at Hiroshima

JAPAN

K. Tange: Municipal Administrative Headquarters at Tokyo

JAPAN

K. Tange: Assembly Hall at Shizuoka

JAPAN

K. Tange: Assembly Hall at Shizuoka

JAPAN

K. Tange: Centre of Peace at Hiroshima

JAPAN